Biblical Models of Handling Conflict

Biblical Models of Handling Conflict

Roy D. Bell

REGENT COLLEGE PUBLISHING
VANCOUVER

BIBLICAL MODELS OF HANDLING CONFLICT
Copyright © 1987 by Roy D. Bell

Original edition published 1987,
by Welch Publishing Company Inc.
960 The Gateway, Burlington, Ontario.
(ISBN 1-55011-026-8)

Reprinted 2001 by Regent College Publishing,
an imprint of the Regent College Bookstore,
5800 University Boulevard, Vancouver, B.C. Canada V6T 2E4
www.regentpublishing.com

Cover illustration by Karen Crigger
Edited by Lloyd Mackey

Views expressed in works published by Regent College Publishing are
those of the author and may not necessarily represent the official
position of Regent College.

Printed in the United States of America

National Library of Canada Cataloguing in Publication Data

Bell, Roy D.
  Biblical models of handling conflict

  ISBN 1-55361-023-7 (Canada)
  ISBN 1-57383-030-5 (U.S.A.)

  1. Conflict management—Religious aspects—Christianity.
2. Christian life. I. Title.
BV4597.53.C58B44 2001   248.4   C2001-910410-3

*To Elizabeth
whose love for the
Word has enriched
all who know her.*

CONTENTS

FOREWORD

The greatest values in life are relational. In fact, the two great commandments of Jesus are to love God and to love our neighbour.

So, obviously, our greatest problems fall in the relational area. Tension, conflict, misunderstanding and the lack of communication are only too well known to all of us.

This book is a prescription that we all should read and meditate upon. Its insights are profound and we will be the richer for having considered them.

Perhaps my greatest motivation for having read this book and in now recommending it to you is that I know Dr. Roy Bell personally.

I respect Roy as much as I respect anyone in Canada today. He is well-read, broadly experienced, and highly articulate. Yet he is down-to-earth and in touch with people of our world.

He was the first guest I chose for our television program over twelve years ago and is still one of our most popular guests. When he discusses Christian issues they come alive and in the final analysis you have confidence in his conclusion.

We became friends almost instantly when we met.

He will become your friend as soon as you begin to read this book. So read it carefully, as if you were listening to Roy talk. That's what this book is—a series of Roy's sermons on friendship, relationships and dealing with conflicts.

Dr. Terry Winter

INTRODUCTION

Conflict has become an ugly word for many people. It reminds us of scenes we see on television showing grisly events like car bombings in Beirut or Belfast. We live in a world where conflict has produced violence which maims, disfigures and destroys people. We have the feeling our world is out of control because of unresolved conflict.

But much of the conflict we experience is significantly more personal. Most of us are familiar with family discord, ranging from the extremes of physical and sexual violence to the more usual quarrels, arguments and verbal abuse—or even silence or withdrawal.

We may not be able to do much about Beirut or Belfast, but we can do something about our own attitudes to conflict; how we deal with it and how we make it productive in our relationships—instead of the opposite.

Many of my earliest memories of family and church were of unresolved conflict. Indeed, it was not simply unresolved; it was unrecognized. Even when I was a child, I felt that there must be a better way to work things out. Some of the people around me coped with conflict either through open anger or rejection. Or they handled it with silence, a method I see now as being even worse.

Through the years, I have looked at conflict from two perspectives.

One way was to observe how major characters in the Bible behaved when they were in crisis. I have found this to be a fascinating study. The characters studied have included such people as Rehoboam and Elijah.

Rehoboam, the son and grandson of Solomon and David respectively, handled conflict by acting tough. He "turned up the heat." It did not work. In our first chapter we will find out why.

Elijah was quite different. Even though he was a godly man, we learn that, at one point, he took off and ran. In our second chapter we will find out whether that worked.

In my studies, I discovered that the ways of dealing with conflict were as varied as the people caught up in the conflicts. Looking further into the Bible, I found that Jesus was an ideal model in the handling of conflict. In many ways, his public ministry involved a series of conflicts. They ranged from minor items, like the dispute with his mother over the wine at the Cana wedding, to the fierce life-and-death struggle with Satan in Gethsemane.

I am convinced that within the pages of the Bible we can find clear examples of how not to handle conflict. In addition, we find excellent biblical principles for helping us to resolve conflict in ways that help us to live life more effectively. We cannot live successfully unless we learn to deal with conflict.

Conflict does not have to be ugly and destructive.

Yet, as I observe conflict in both my own activities and in the lives of others, it often emerges as something to avoid or to use as a demonstration of power over someone else. This has led me to look at what conflict does to people. In so doing, my concern is not so much with the extremes which leave people open to criminal charges, but with the more common kinds of conflict which produce discouragement, disillusionment and, sometimes, even despair. Solomon's Song refers to the little foxes which spoil the vines. Relationships which, under God, could be rich and productive go sour because the way we cope with conflict often results in the opposite of what we intend. These results could come from deliberate sins—or from causes of which we are not aware.

I recognize that most of us feel we can do without conflict or tension. It does bad things to us—and it also causes us to do bad things to others. It is hard to know which is the worst. Though we want to do without conflict, that wish will not make it disappear.

It wears us out both emotionally and physically. It also causes us to wear out the people who are most important to us. The result is that too much of our energy is being used up negatively.

It wears us out emotionally, sometimes, because we keep repeating the agenda that bothers us. While we may do that repetition out loud, more often it is likely that we carry it out internally. We debate with ourselves and it wears us out. We become depressed, which is bad news for us, or we become angry, which is bad news for everybody else.

Different people react differently to tension. Some of us become "hyper." We become so wound up that we cannot stop ourselves from talking about the thing which makes us angry.

Other people become exhausted. They feel tired and defeated. I am sure you can recognize this in yourself and in others.

Tension can affect us spiritually, too, because all our energy goes into the issue in which we are involved, whether it be family, political or our reaction to a world situation. When all our energy goes to such tense issues, our spiritual resources are depleted . . . spent . . . wasted . . . and gone.

Yes, most of us believe we could do without conflict. We would prefer that it happen only occasionally. Yet conflict is a normal part of life.

Indeed, some would argue that in many cases, tension and conflict are the best evidences that we are alive. Others would want some more positive evidence of life!

Hans Selye, a Montrealer who has done more than most to open up the subject of stress and conflict, describes it as the "spice of life."

Someone else, however, has described stress as the greatest killer.

How do we reconcile these two positions?

Could it be that the issue is not so much in the conflict or tension itself, but in how I deal with it?

In this book, I hope we can look at how the Bible handles this issue and how we can apply Biblical teaching to our own lives.

Some of the models we will look at are very effective. They have resulted in life-changing, spiritually-liberating possibilities in the lives of individuals. They have meant significant breakthroughs for the people experiencing the tension as well as for the lives of others touched by those people.

We will also look at some ineffective—or even destructive—models.

Ironically, the period which will be the subject of this study has cast its shadow down the centuries, even to the news of this very day. It has been an arena of conflict which, even today, threatens not only the lives of those in the Middle East, but the rest of the world as well.

Learning how to recognize and resolve conflict, for such nations, would have changed the very course of their history. We can have, at least, the more modest goal, that of learning to recognize and resolve conflict in a way which glorifies God, bringing release and joy to our relationships.

In starting this study, I would encourage you not to ask God to stop the conflict in your life. The more you pray, the more you desire a conflict-free life, the more pressure conflict will exert.

I would encourage you to pray for the Spirit who can give you understanding of the nature of your conflicts. In these studies, we will aim to understand conflict and to understand ourselves as we face conflict.

When we achieve such understanding, we achieve breakthrough and real change in life.

NOBODY'S GOING
TO PUSH ME AROUND

Text: I Kings 12:1-15

Rehoboam answered the people harshly. Rejecting the advice given him by the elders, he followed the advice of the young men and said, "My father scourged you with whips; I will scourge you with scorpions." So the king did not listen to the people. (I Kings 12:13-15)

Rehoboam, as Solomon's son and his successor to Israel's throne, knew how to turn up the heat. He was obviously adept at throwing gasoline on the fire. He would show everyone how tough he was. His attitude was, "Nobody's going to push me around!"

Let me try to paint the picture of his behavior and its effect on people, in contemporary terms.

. . . It is late at night. Your phone rings. Your best friend is on the other end of the line. He does not start the conversation with any of the niceties, but, with deep feeling, bursts out, "I am mad at you."

Do you react by exploding at him? "I can be just as tough as he is!" What are the consequences?

. . . You are in your late teens. You are given permission to stay out until 11:00 p.m. You arrive home at 11:10. Before you can explain, your father grounds you.

Do you react by being just as angry? "If he thinks it is okay to treat me like that, I can be just as mean!" What are the consequences?

. . . You are called into your boss' office on a Friday afternoon. Obviously upset, he informs you, "I am sorry, but we cannot afford you any more."

15

Do you respond by telling him what he can do with his job and his sorrow? Who wins?

You arrive home after a busy and stressful day. Your spouse does not give you time to settle down and catch your breath. "We have had a letter from your mother and she wants to come and live with us. You had better make up your mind; it is her or me!"

You are tired. You have been looking forward to a relaxed meal and some peace and quiet. Can you stop before you reply? Can you try to find out what is really going on?

Or, before either of you can get a hold of yourselves, are you in the middle of a blazing row?

In each of these examples—and you can likely supply your own as well—there was no attempt to listen, understand or explain. Both parties to the discussion seemed bent on a power struggle and were out to prove who could dominate. Does either party win when he acts or reacts in those ways?

In this chapter, we can observe the effect of this kind of conflict—particularly that generated by the person who "turned up the heat," the kind of person who is determined that "nobody is going to push me around." In the biblical context, Rehoboam was one such person. We need to see what we can learn from him. That is, to a large extent, what not to do.

Rehoboam was King Solomon's son. He was King David and Bathsheba's grandson, so he came from a famous family. They had celebrity status. He inherited his father's throne. The reigns of David and Solomon had been highlights in the history of Israel. With people like the Queen of Sheba knocking at their doors, they were well aware that they were reigning over the largest empire known until that time.

It was a period marked by an enormous breakthrough in culture, as well. The Psalms, the Proverbs and Ecclesiastes were substantially written during this time—and they represented the flowering of poetry, music and celebration.

As well, there had been spiritual revival in Israel, or at least the appearance of one. During Solomon's reign, the revival was more appearance than reality. Indeed, there were what ultimately proved to be the seeds of decay.

Even today, the people of Israel see this as a most significant period. In Jerusalem, the most famous hotel, for example, is the King David.

But there was a dark side to Solomon's reign, too, and that tends to set the stage for Rehoboam's behavior and actions. It certainly helps us to understand why the confrontation took place.

Solomon reigned for 40 years. When the Queen of Sheba visited him, she pointed out that "in wisdom and wealth, you have far exceeded the report I have heard." While this was true, it was far from the whole truth. It was a one-sided assessment.

Solomon's genius had more to do with his use of words and his legal skills than with his wisdom as a ruler and king. No doubt his fame rested on verbal skills, but that was not enough.

For example, his taxation policies were ruinous. He extracted a yearly tribute of gold from his subjects far beyond their ability to pay. The buildings he constructed were also beyond the resources of the community. Quite rightly, he is credited with building the temple, but his own personal palace was four times the size of the structure he raised to honor the Lord.

This tells us about Solomon's ego. It was clearly larger than his devotion to the Lord. People were over-taxed and over-worked on projects which had far more to do with that ego than they had to do with the social, personal and spiritual needs of the people. Indeed, Solomon had not only become indifferent to spiritual things; he had tolerated and even encouraged practices that he knew to be wrong. He ignored the direct intervention of God, himself (I Kings 11:9, 10).

He had a system of double-taxation. Many of us are convinced Canada has a similar system! Knowing the resentment our own system can generate, we can understand the feelings the people of Israel had toward their king. He taxed all the country heavily except Judah. It would be as if in Canada, Quebec were to be exempt from federal taxes while the rest of Canada paid for extravagant programs carried out there.

The money was being drained from all parts of the nation to pay for extravagance in Jerusalem. Those of us from western Canada know what we think of tax money being drained into Toronto, Ottawa and Montreal!

In his last days, as has been noted, Solomon departed from his loyalty to the Lord. The Bible tells us he loved many foreign women: women from nations with which God had forbidden the people of Israel to intermarry "because surely they will turn your hearts to their gods" (I Kings 11:2). It was not so much that they were non-Israelites; after all, David's grandmother was Ruth, a Moabite woman. The difficulty with these women was that their loyalty was not to the Lord.

Solomon had 700 wives of royal birth, plus 300 mistresses. We should hardly be surprised that he was led astray! There are other things which cause us to wander, as well!

It was the effect of this side of Solomon which set up the confrontation with Rehoboam. The representatives of the people came to him with the intention of making him king. They said to him, "Your father treated us unjustly. Now if you treat us justly, we will serve you." It is true that this was a clear challenge. Given the circumstances, however, it was reasonable—and there was room for negotiation and settlement.

There are three things to note about the way Rehoboam responded to the peoples' approach to him. The process he followed was not all bad.

1. He asked for a little time so he could seek advice. In the intervening three days he took counsel from the well respected elders as well as from some of the younger people. He sought balanced advice, a wise route to follow in a situation of potential conflict. It must be admitted, though, that he appeared to be looking for the advice which he was determined to follow in the first place.

Often, in conflict, the people whose advice we seek are the people we know will support us in what we want to do. At least we can give Rehoboam credit for finding counsellors representative of two viewpoints, not just his own.

2. He did not attempt to deny the truth of the allegations of the people, with respect to his father's behavior. He listened and did not deny. He did not dispute the facts.

He resisted the temptation to deny or argue when the facts were clear. He deserves credit for that as well, though his listening skills were inadequate.

3. Rehoboam recognized he was dealing with political and

power concerns. Unfortunately, he did not deal with them by trying to discover what was right, biblical or godly. For him, the question to be answered was, "Who will rule?" rather than, "What is God's will?" He was concerned with power and the domination of others. He had no thought for a settlement that would serve the people who confronted him.

Rehoboam had little thought for the consequences and seemed to have little sense of the fact that the kingdom belonged to God, not to him. He appears to have been blind to everything except his ability to demonstrate that "Nobody is going to push me around."

In conflict, we need to recognize that the bottom line for the Christian is never, "How can I get my own way?" but rather, "How will the Lord be honored?" When we forget that, we become destructive, with little thought for reconciliation. Indeed, reconciliation becomes impossible.

Rehoboam had no thought about the good of the people he was supposed to serve. His approach to resolving the conflict was to

. . . TURN UP THE HEAT.

"I will show them," he was saying. "My father scourged you with whips. I will scourge you with scorpions."

He took the advice of the younger people rather than the elders. He said that if Solomon's yoke was heavy, his would be heavier. In addition, the Bible notes, "The king did not listen to the people."

It is clear, both from this biblical passage and from the most casual observation of life, that the failure to listen is a critical issue. It pervades all our failures in relationships. Present day psychologists, on the other hand, encourage *primary level accurate empathy* in personal counselling.

This is a listening skill. Empathy means to attempt to get inside the feelings, convictions and words of the person with whom you are in contact. Primary level accurate empathy encourages the counsellor not to offer advice at that point, but to confirm with the other person that your understanding is accurate.

Rehoboam listened, not to understand, but to debate, to rebut, to react—and, in the end, to terminate any hope of reconciliation.

It is hard to listen, but no conflict will ever be resolved constructively without real listening.

It is tempting to speculate why Rehoboam did not listen. Was it just anxiety for himself? Was he telling himself, "If I do not show how tough I am, they will walk all over me?" Or was he simply exhibiting pride and arrogance? The evidence would appear to favor the latter.

If only Rehoboam had learned to listen—really listen. Not only would his personal history have been different, but also that of his nation.

Failure to listen is always the first roadblock to resolving conflict. How quick we are to respond; how slow to hear. James is most wise when he writes, "Everyone should be quick to listen, slow to speak and slow to become angry."

Are you a listener or just a reactor?

In turning up the heat, Rehoboam ignored what the Lord had to say and sought, instead, to resolve conflict in a carnal and destructive fashion. He fell into the trap many of us do when faced with such a situation; he failed to listen and he put his own ego first. There can be no surer way to produce disaster than such a combination.

Unfortunately, it is almost normal to proceed in such a fashion. We may plead anxiety or feel the need to exercise authority. Whichever action we take, the result is the same; the opportunity for reconciliation is missed. As in Rehoboam's case, the problem which could have been solved so easily becomes a mess it never needed to be.

Whatever the causes, this manner of dealing with conflict is both sinful and destructive. What a combination!

How could we think that by turning up the heat and putting on more pressure, we could resolve an issue in our favor. Even if we get our way in these circumstances, resentment is created which, in the end, destroys whatever temporary victory we may appear to have won. Each person, in seeking his or her own self-interest, ignores what the Lord is saying.

That is the kind of response Rehoboam engendered. I Kings 12:16 notes that when he refused to listen to the people, they invoked the revered name of his grandfather, David, noting in frustration, "What share do we have in David?" Rejection was becoming complete.

The attitude of "nobody is going to push me around" temporarily satisfies one's own ego, but destroys everything else.

Is that your way of resolving conflict? If so, you must have noticed that everybody loses.

Rehoboam was determined to have a power struggle, no matter the cost.

Power struggles admittedly are sometimes inevitable. This is so when reality forces us to recognize that all other ways of solving problems have been exhausted. It cannot be the first method of resolving conflict.

Woe to the person who pursues the power struggle without justification from the Lord, simply for the sake of winning for themselves! That person brings tragedy, sickness and sadness all the way down the line. He or she becomes a one-person wrecking team.

Some of us become easily locked into power struggles. Some families have individuals whose normal way of relating to others is through such power struggles. I refer not to normal family give and take, but to the situation where people use power struggles to force other family members to do their will.

How well I remember the power struggles of my childhood. Nobody won. Nobody. Whenever I have rushed into a power struggle in personal relationships, I have always lost. Even when I have won, I have lost, through the hurt I have created, the resentment I have stirred up and the care and love I have disrupted.

I would reiterate; it is not always possible to avoid a power struggle. Indeed, it is desirable to engage in them: otherwise the very convictions the Bible asserts can be lost. But they are the last resort, not the first.

Too often, power struggles are seen as a first resort. This is particularly true in family life. A marriage which begins so full of promise breaks up. While there are all kinds of explanations, one major cause relates to unresolved power struggles. Neither spouse knows how to recognize what they are getting into—or how to step out before the struggle devours them.

At least you can make a beginning, by asking yourself if that is how it is for you. Those silly arguments about trivial issues are sapping all the gentleness out of the relationship. Why is it so important for you to win? Why do you have to have your own way? Why can't you listen to the distress and violation which is happening? In your endeavour to prove that nobody is going to push you around, you end up losing what is most precious in your life. You become the person who does to others what you cannot stand being done to you.

How can any of this glorify God?

How can any of this enrich your life?

We do well to remember that, in family life, all of us have power. Each family member has a different kind of power—like the power deriving from earning a living or handling the budget. The real issue is not whether you have power but how you use it.

"But you don't understand," someone responds. "I don't have any power." Ralph Nader, as I understand it, did not earn as much as any General Motors assembly line worker, yet he revolutionized that major American industry. He had power. You may have power, even if you lack financial clout or physical authority.

In most families, power has nothing to do with money but rather with love and affection given or withheld. The most powerful people in such families are those on whom others depend for the meeting of their needs.

In some families, for example, members who feel they are powerless withhold affection or dump anger on other members. Such examples illustrate the fact that the issue is not simply the availability of power but the exercise of it.

Do you excercise power in your family in that fashion?

Sometimes, the so-called "powerless" person dominates the family by creating an atmosphere which leaves no time or space for love or care.

Clearly it is desirable, in every area of human life, to be aware that power struggles are undesirable. If Rehoboam, for example, had been prepared to ask himself and others, "Why are the people angry?" he would have quickly discerned the answer—and the possibility of reconciliation would have emerged. He never did that. He made no attempt to discover their concerns, or what caused them. The results were predictably calamitous.

To take the trouble to discover why the conflict is happening . . . to try finding out what the real concerns are . . . to begin to hear each other out without being angry . . . is surely to make a constructive beginning.

The major matter is to learn from this incident. Can you make a beginning? Will you ask the Lord to help you?

When you find yourself in the middle of conflict, could you stop and ask yourself the questions like:

"What is really going on?"

"Am I simply determined to get my own way?"

"Am I really listening to all that is being communicated?"

"Am I into the kind of power struggle in which the matter at issue is not as important the fact that I really want to win?"

"Do I even care what the Lord would have me do?"

Will you ask yourself, "What is the grievance in this relationship which causes me to react as I do? What goes on inside me that I know I would like God to change?" Will you leave aside the inappropriateness of the other person's behavior and look at how you are reacting?

Conflict, tension, stress and power struggles are normal parts of living. We are easily locked into them. When you sense you are locked in, you need to ask yourself: "How can I glorify God in this situation?"

When you begin to see that conflict is a normal part of living, you can start accepting it as such. When you begin to find yourself locked into destructive conflict which is destroying precious relationships, it is time to take a fresh look at how you cope with conflict.

If you are like Rehoboam, you will need urgently to change. You will find yourself in serious circumstances if you do not. The relationships you hold dear will become troubled and eventually will die. Love, gentleness, belonging: all these and more will begin to depart from your life. It will leave you angry, bewildered, resentful and turn you into a person without real intimacy. In the end, it will spill out into your relationship with God, whom you will too easily blame for what were your own choices.

Rehoboam and his nation never really recovered. The kingdom split and became an easy prey to its enemies.

Rehoboam lost authority and the very power he sought to demonstrate.

He could have listened. He could have sought and discovered what his people's concerns were. He could have stepped back from his determination not to be "pushed around." He could have, but he did not.

Who but a fool wants to be a Rehoboam? The alternatives can so easily lead to reconciliation, deeper love and care, a sense of bonding and belonging.

Under God, I will not be such a person as Rehoboam. Under God, instead of turning up the heat, I will get out of the power struggle. Not only will I listen to others, but be open to what the Holy Spirit will teach me.

When those changes take place in your life, you enter into a lifestyle and a way of relating to others which is life-changing and liberating. The things you feared you would lose become the things you gain. You enter into a measure of peace, joy and good relationships which is infinitely and deeply satisfying.

RUNNING AWAY:
THE YEARN TO ESCAPE

I Kings 19

Now Ahab told Jezebel everything Elijah had done and how he had killed all the prophets with the sword. So Jezebel sent a messenger to Elijah to say, "May the gods deal with me, be it ever so severely, if by this time tomorrow I do not make your life like that of one of them."
Elijah was afraid and ran for his life.
When he came to Beersheba in Judah, he left his servant there, while he himself went a day's journey into the desert. He came to a broom tree, sat down under it and prayed that he might die. "I have had enough, Lord," he said. "Take my life; I am no better than my ancestors." (I Kings 19:1-4)

Jezebel, the wife of Ahab the King was quite a person, certainly not the type one would love or trust. She was wicked. Her masterminding of the murder of Naboth, in order to get his vineyard, demonstrates her wickedness. She was a violent, unscrupulous, immoral and amoral person.

Nevertheless, you have to admire her nerve.

Elijah had confronted Jezebel's protégés, the prophets of Baal, utterly and totally defeating and destroying them.

One would have expected her to be dismayed, even confused and disoriented in the wake of that defeat. Not Jezebel.

She immediately sent a message to Elijah, who had been so victorious, informing him that he was done for. She was very cool. It is difficult to find a contemporary equivalent. Would her action have been like that of Napoleon, writing a threatening letter to Wellington after being sent into exile at St. Helene? Or Colonel Gadhafi blustering after the Americans bombed Libya?

25

The astonishing factor in Jezebel's action was not so much her message but Elijah's reaction. He fell apart. He totally collapsed. He took off and fled.

At first sight, his action made no sense at all: the victorious Elijah falling apart in a situation of minor conflict with Jezebel. In an emotional sense, it was like falling from the top of the CN Tower or the Empire State Building.

Clearly, Elijah's reaction to this particular conflict was complex. His swift rush to the bottom of the roller coaster was not normal for him. Yet fall he did: from victory, to defeat, to emotional collapse, all in less than 24 hours.

It is too easy to say that this kind of reaction is normal. There was something more extreme happening to Elijah. It would appear accurate to diagnose his condition as adrenalin depletion. This would provide some way of understanding how sudden and complete was his collapse. Archibald Hart of Fuller Theological Seminary has written extensively and wisely on this subject.[1] In those terms, it is understandable that Elijah was as strung out as he was.

All of us, in minor ways, have these kinds of experiences. You may recall having had an exciting, yet stressful day, then waking up the next morning feeling low. There may have been a nameless feeling of dread or loss. It does not make sense in terms of the exciting things which have gone on before. You believe you ought to be on top of the world but, in fact, things are on top of you. The cause may simply be adrenaline depletion.

But, there were other facets to Elijah's problems.

There was his fear of Jezebel. Did he fear her because she was a woman? Hardly. More likely his feelings derived from her strong personality and the things she stood for. Jezebel was not just an evil and wicked person. In many ways she was the manifestation of evil itself. The prophets of Baal were the servants of evil; in some ways, she was the incarnation of evil.

It may be that Elijah felt himself to be in conflict with evil itself.

According to the godly standards set in the Old Testament,

---

1. Hart, Archibald, *Adrenalin and Stress*, Word, 1986.

Jezebel should not have been the wife of Ahab. The difficulty was not simply her ethnic background; it was a question of her religious commitment. The Bible did not rule out marriage of an Israelite and non-Israelite. One good and famous example was that of Ruth and Boaz, the grandparents of David. The objection to a woman of Jezebel's background was religious and spiritual, not ethnic or racial.

Jezebel's father was king of the Sidonians. He was the priest of Ashtoroth, the Sidonian goddess of sexual love, maternity and fertility. That, at first sight, seems innocent enough. Sexual love, maternity and fertility are hardly seen as evil in the Bible. Indeed, they are celebrated in the entire Song of Solomon.

What is wrong, then, with the Ashtoroth perspective?

A great deal. The whole of Sidonian society was dominated by a philosophy which finds contemporary expression in Playboy, Penthouse and Hustler—and degenerates from there.

In our terms, the Sidonian philosophy provided the whole justification for legal prostitution and all kinds of sexual self-indulgence. It had a debasing effect on moral responsibility and behavior.

Through Jezebel's influence, this philosophy was being given the sanction of law and religion within the nation of Israel. Prostitution is an evil, not only because of the sexual implications, but because it treats a human being—the prostitute—as something to be bought, used and discarded at the impulse of the person seeking out that human being.

Yet, then as now, Baal worship seemed much more attractive than the values and convictions of the Bible. Jezebel and her allies promoted self-indulgence while Elijah and his fellow prophets argued for self-denial. It is so easy to buy into the Playboy/Baal view of life. It appears attractive. It seduces us. The opposite seems hard, austere, asking more of us than we want to give.

Can you understand why the Israelites found the appeal of Baal and Jezebel such a magnet? It promised so much: warmth, excitement, glamor and sexual satisfaction. All these appeared available for the asking; never mind that in the long run they did not deliver. Those who were seduced said the failure to deliver was tomorrow's problem—and who knows about tomorrow? All we have is today.

Few of us, then, would have difficulty in understanding why the struggle for the soul of Israel was so intense.

It is tempting to believe that the best course of action might be promiscuity or self-indulgence—taking what you want because it feels good. "I want it. I must have it. How can it be so bad when it feels so good?" These and other similar thoughts enter our minds.

The conflicting values which Jezebel introduced to Ahab and his people are clearly similar to the conflicting values Christians face in this latter part of the 20th century. Ahab and Jezebel were on one end of the spectrum; Elijah was on the other.

Which end do you find yourself on, right now? Either one or the other . . . or in point of fact, both?

That is why Elijah says to the people of Israel, in I Kings 18:21, "How long will you waver between two opinions? If the Lord be God, follow him; if Baal, follow him."

They wanted the Lord and they also wanted to follow Baal.

In fact, Elijah is not speaking to the issue of choice, but pointing out that the people were trying to combine the worship of Baal and of Jehovah.

Has very much really changed?

That point is pertinent to us, today. Frequently, we try to keep our feet in both camps. We try to covet the Playboy philosophy on one hand and the worship of Jesus Christ on the other. This produces all kinds of internal conflicts, ending up with the worst of both worlds, rather than the best.

We try to keep both options open. The attempt to live in both worlds makes us dissatisfied and angry with life itself. This unresolved conflict curses our lives.

In telling the people to choose rather than merge, Elijah created a real fight. Out of that fight came a great victory for Jehovah. In the aftermath, Jezebel exercised the considerable nerve I referred to earlier, sending Elijah a very intimidating message. She tells him that she expects her gods to deal with her severely if she does not deal Elijah the same fate as that of the slain prophets of Baal—within 24 hours.

Under that kind of intimidation, Elijah ran away.

Despite his faithfulness to Jehovah, his courage and his moral uprightness, he couldn't take Jezebel's threat. He had won the battle and God had vindicated himself by sending down the fire on the water-soaked altar built in his honor. But just a word from Jezebel unhinged him.

What was wrong with Elijah?

Before we tackle that question, let us take note of what was not wrong with him.

He was not *manic depressive*—a man with violent mood swings. If you are a person with violent mood swings, it is important to know simply that no matter how your moods swing, the Lord remains the same. It may also be important to accept medication. Mood swings represent a serious problem, but that was not what was wrong with Elijah.

In addition, Elijah's prayer, asking for his own death, *was not totally out of the ordinary.*

Haven't you ever felt like that, like you have had enough? Have you ever wanted to tell God, "Don't you know what it is like to be me, to be under all this pressure, and now this? I can't take any more. Enough is enough."

Elijah's prayer reflects some things about the Bible which sometimes escape our attention.

I love the Bible because of its humanity, its reality and its emotion, as well as because of its conviction and teaching. Elijah was not the first servant of God who had wanted to die. So had Job . . . and Moses . . . and Jonah.

Some of you know exactly how Elijah was feeling. While he did not commit suicide as a result of his conflict and depression, he felt like it. "I have had enough, Lord . . . take my life."

I don't blame Elijah for his feelings. It is important to notice that the Lord did not condemn him, either. It would be an understatement to say that blame is unhelpful; to be depressed is bad enough. To have someone add God's condemnation could be to push that person to the edge. It is contrary to Scripture's way of dealing with those feelings.

The Bible always handles depression with reassurance, not condemnation. We had better learn to do the same. Whatever blame to be assigned to Elijah's reaction belongs to Jezebel. The reality is evident.

Elijah had a king-sized depression. He handled it by running away.

The 20th century equivalent to Elijah's action is summed up in what you mean if you say, "Stop the world, I want to get off."

You may run away by staying where you are and withdrawing into yourself, so nobody knows what is going on inside your head.

Or you may run away as Elijah did, by running physically as hard and as fast as he could.

Running away may be either an emotional or a physical means of responding to depression.

Elijah could no longer tolerate the situation in which he found himself, despite his victory.

I am not sure if Elijah felt that running away would solve anything. I suspect he ran away for the obvious reason. He could not take any more pressure.

His action may have been irrational and useless, but "enough was enough." The combination of adrenalin depletion and the sudden challenge of evil represented by Jezebel produced a king-sized depression. Elijah took off.

He ran for his life.

In our society, we are often not permitted to acknowledge our depression. Furthermore, we often do not understand depression as it manifests itself, either in ourselves or others. On the surface, it does not always make sense. At first sight, Elijah's depression made no sense. Whether it makes sense or not, however, it is there; it needs to be understood and it needs help.

Depression means more than simply feeling down, blue and discouraged. While those feelings are part of it, we recognize that depression can also involve a sense that *there is no longer any meaning to life*. There may be no logic to such feelings but they are there. "I have everything a person could want but it all seems so pointless."

Depression can also mean a *loss of energy, drive and the desire to accomplish*. You can recall having once gone about your life with gusto, but now no more. It has become boring, repetitious and bland. "I no longer have any goals and if I did have there would be no energy to pursue them."

Depression affects people of all ages. In point of fact, in our kind of society, it has become chronic with many young people. It is one of the most common factors leading to teen suicide. It has reached epidemic proportions in many places. Canada and the United States together, so I am told, has a larger proportion of teen suicide than a country like Japan, where it has been seen as critical.

This biblical passage does not deal comprehensively with depression and certainly not with suicide. It focuses on a particular issue relating to depression—the desire to escape, to run away. But it does remind us of depression's reality and sees it as arising out of conflict.

Are there any of us who can honestly say that they are never depressed. People have various ways of handling depression, however. Elijah handled it, if that is the proper word, by withdrawal.

There would appear to have been one more factor in the way Elijah reacted to the conflict with Jezebel. He had lost contact with the godly community. The Lord had to tell him, "Yet I reserve 7,000 in Israel—all whose knees have not bowed down to Baal and all whose mouths have not kissed him."

Obviously, there was a significant support group available to Elijah that he either did not know or did not contact.

Could it be that this failure meant a far deeper sense of "being lost" than was necessary?

It certainly increased his feelings of disillusionment and betrayal. He twice says to God "I am the only one left, and now they are trying to kill me, too."

It is clear that all of us need support systems. We may very well need them just as much when all is going well, as when things are going badly. Without such support systems, much goes by the board. There is no one with whom to share the good news, let alone the bad. The support system may fail us at times, even as we ourselves fail, but its very existence is essential to our spiritual and emotional health.

God reminds Elijah of this. Do you need a similar reminder?

His support group existed to pray for him and with him.

Why do we neglect such a resource? Elijah's backup was there to support him in the conflict with Baal and Jezebel but he chose to "go it alone." He was physically and, seemingly, spiritually alone.

Is it any wonder that Elijah fell apart?

Here he was, locked into a conflict that drained him physically and emotionally. He was being directly opposed by the evil one. He was up against a seductive and erotic religion. Added to all that, he had cut himself off from any support system.

No wonder Elijah wanted to die. No wonder he took off. He even memorized that prayer of complaint referred to earlier. Twice he tells God, "I have been very zealous for the Lord God. The Israelites have rejected your covenant, broken down your altars and put your prophets to the sword. I am the only one left and now they are trying to kill me, too."

So in Elijah's depression, there were chemical, psychological, physical and spiritual issues—all intertwined. Elijah was "burned out," as we say today. And, like 20th century people who are burned out, he was not particularly attractive or enjoyable.

Burned-out people are of strong commitment and conviction who have cut themselves off from their support systems. That is what Elijah had done. If you follow the same pattern, you will find yourself in the same position.

While there is much to be said about the dangers of stress and burnout, one thing is clear; those who end up burned out are always committed people—of a particular kind. Their problem is not so much their overt dedication as their failure to listen and be supported by people with whom they have deep and intimate relationships. Cutting yourself off from community, in that sense, means there is no buffer between you and disaster.

Fortunately, both for Elijah and ourselves, that is not the end of it.

What exactly did God do about the consequences of Elijah's conflict and its fallout?

God ministered to Elijah physically. He provided rest and refreshment for him. The text tells us that an angel touched him and said to get up and eat. He looked around and there, beside his head, was a hot loaf of bread and a jar of water. He ate and drank, then lay down again, having had his immediate needs met by his God.

God did not preach a sermon to Elijah on the subject of depression. He did not tell him he ought to be ashamed of himself. He did not scold, blame, rebuke or complain. He ministered to him physically and emotionally. I think that is marvellous. What a difference from the way we would have reacted. No sermons! No appeals for dedication or rededication!

God gave Elijah time and space. He saw that Elijah needed renewal and space, so he gave him 40 days and 40 nights. He did not expect him to recover immediately. There was no instant change from calamity to praise. That would come, but right now, the process which required time had begun.

God allowed Elijah to spill out verbally the things that were bothering him. Even though what Elijah said was inaccurate and inappropriate, he allowed him to tell what was troubling him.

He lets him "vent his spleen" not once, but twice.

Even though what Elijah said was not true, God does not tell him to "let me get your facts straight for you." It is marvelous to see how God deals with Elijah—not with impatience, anger and resentment, as we would. Instead of making his problem worse, God listens to Elijah.

The graciousness of God is mind-boggling. He modifies Elijah's perception of reality. He then lets him know what he is to do, reminding him that there are still 7,000 who have not bowed the knee to Baal.

Sometimes, we need to have God modify our perception of reality. We are convinced that no one loves us and everyone hates us. We want to go and eat worms. Then, having heard us out, God gently reminds us that we are not perceiving the real truth.

He tells us, "I love you and there are other people who love you, if you will let them. You do not have to eat worms; there is a better diet available." God has modified our perception of reality.

God gave Elijah an assignment. He gave him work to do. He told him to go back the way he came, anoint two kings and commission his own successor. He was to anoint Hazael king over Arma and Jehu, king of Israel. He was to anoint Elisha as his prophet successor.

By providing Elisha, God not only provided Elijah with part of an assignment, but gave him the beginnings of an additional support system.

Above and beyond all that, he revealed himself to Elijah. He did so in a way that filled Elijah with awe and wonder.

One of the Bible's most moving passages runs from verse 11 to verse 13. God tells Elijah to "stand on the mountain in the presence of the Lord."

A great wind passed by, tearing the mountains apart and shattering the rocks—but the Lord was not in the wind.

An earthquake came, but the Lord was not in the earthquake.

A fire came, but the Lord was not in the fire.

Then came a *gentle whisper.* When Elijah heard it, he pulled his cloak over his face and went out into the mouth of the cave where he had hidden himself. The Lord was in that gentle whisper; and Elijah broke through to what John Sherrill describes as "an overwhelming sense of the presence of God" in his life.

Isn't God's goodness marvelous? How special he is! How much he cares for you and for me!

When conflict is so severe that it leads us into depression, we don't need to be afraid of depression and mood change. They are not signs that God doesn't love you or that you do not love God. We so easily come to believe such errors.

Don't allow your reactions to persuade you that God is indifferent to you and your needs. He is not.

Don't neglect the obvious physical and emotional factors which contribute to depression. They need to be recognized and dealt with.

Above all, do not count God out.

God saw Elijah through and he will see you through. You do not have to run away. There are better solutions. Running away is futile because you take yourself along.

God met Elijah at every point of his need. He did not fob him off with a pile of pious platitudes. He ministered to him at depth. At every point of Elijah's breakdown, God was there.

He met his physical needs with rest and food.

He changed his perception of what was going on by reminding him of the facts.

He reassured him of His majesty and faithfulness.

He restored him to the beginnings of community.

He gave him useful work to do and provided the resources to do it.

Conflict can be so severe, at times, that it seems to demolish us and make us despair of everything. It can have many causes and many consequences.

God ministers to us in the midst of it all. He teaches us about ourselves and Himself. He stays with us in the despair and sees us through.

Let Him do that for you.

Hear that gentle whisper which will help you begin to know again of his care.

It can lead us to the kind of assurance that Walter Rauschenbusch wrote about in the following words:

> When I enter into God
> All life has a meaning,
> Without asking I know,
> My desires are even now fulfilled
>
> My fever is gone
> In the great quiet of God
> My troubles are but pebbles on the road,
> My joys are like the everlasting hills.

SEEING THE UNSEEN

II Kings 6:8-24

And Elisha prayed, "O Lord, open his eyes so he may see."
Then the Lord opened the servant's eyes and he looked and saw
the hills full of horses and chariots of fire all around Elisha. (II
Kings 6:17)

The story behind this text is straightforward. The happenings surrounding Elisha's comments and prayer, however, are electrifying and not nearly as simple.

The king of Aram (Syria) had a problem. Somebody appeared to be betraying his military movements to his enemy, the king of Israel. He complained with outrage, "Will you not tell me which of us is on the side of the king of Israel?"

Twentieth century nations may use spying techniques much more sophisticated than those of Elisha's day. We have our Philbys; the Americans, their Walkers and Whitworths. In Canada, the case of Herbert Norman and the Hambleton affair continues to generate controversy. Nevertheless, spying has been a way of life for millennia.

But the case in this passage is much more unusual.

The chapter tells us that Elisha, the prophet, was the villain—so to speak. "Elisha, the prophet, who is in Israel, tells the king of Israel the very words you speak in your bedroom." So repeated the king's advisors.

That is quite a shocker—in more ways than one!

The king of Aram did not doubt the truth of the allegations. He sent an army to Dothan to collect Elisha. (I wonder why the king thought Elisha would not know about that!)

When Elisha and his servant woke up in the morning, "an army with horses and chariots had surrounded the city." Understandably, Elisha's servant was frightened, crying out,

"Oh my lord, what shall we do?"

Who could blame him?

He could see the enemy and nothing else. He found himself in the midst of an armed conflict and it dominated his perception of reality.

Nothing and nobody existed for Elisha's servant but the size and ferocity of the forces against him.

Does that sound familiar?

So many of us are like Elisha's servant. What we see, within limitations, is accurate, but we are not able to focus beyond those limitations. We see the conflict. We fear the enemy, but we do not see—nor do we rely on—the sovereign hand of the Lord.

In response to Elisha's prayer, "the Lord opened the servant's eyes and he looked and saw the hills full of horses and chariots of fire all around Elisha." This was an unseen support system.

The prophet then reminded his servant, "Don't be afraid . . . those who are with us are more than those who are with them."

Many of us are like Elisha's servant. We see superficially. We do not see what is there to be seen by the eyes of faith. Or, we reject the idea of eyes of faith as pious talk and nothing more.

When we first came to Canada, I remember being in a small Baptist Church in the Maritimes. Coming out of the service, I recall seeing the early October colors of the magnificent valley lying before me. As I feasted on the sight of the deep red maples and the other brilliant hues, I said to a member of the congregation, "Isn't it beautiful?" A lifelong resident of the valley, she replied, "I suppose so. I never noticed it."

What do you see?

The story is told of a British painter by the name of Constable. He painted old-fashioned landscapes and was especially adept at painting a thunderstorm with the light shining through the dark clouds.

One evening, while he was painting a sunset, someone looked over his shoulder at the painting, then at the sunset. The observer said to Constable, "I don't see that," to which the painter replied, "Don't you wish you did?"

What do you see?

Some people see only life's problems, its darkness and despair. Others see joy, wonder, splendor and beauty. What makes the difference?

The difference obviously is critical. Far too many people see only the negatives. They are surrounded by conflict. They perceive only the problems; they are paralyzed and embittered by them.

What do we see?

Sir Walter Scott and Lord Byron were respected and admired 19th century British writers. In addition to being literary figures, they had something else in common. Both were lame and were less than fully mobile.

Byron, some of his biographers note, was skeptical, cynical and critical. At age 34, he wrote:

My days are in the sear and yellow leaf,
The flowers and the fruit of life are gone.
The worm, the canker and the grief are mine
Alone.

Byron, it seems, fought adversity all his life, with little success.

Scott, on the other hand, never lost his joy and radiance. That condition prevailed despite the fact that his publishers went bankrupt. He spent much of his life paying debts he had not personally incurred, rather than receiving the financial benefits his talents should have afforded him.

The difference between Byron and Scott, the reason some people see beyond failure and limitation and others do not, is the issue behind this particular biblical passage.

Before we explore those differences, however, I would like to parenthetically deal with the role of prophecy and the prophets in the Old Testament.

Elijah and Elisha, the people whose lives are explored in the books of the Kings, introduced what is called the "rise of prophecy" in the Bible. They were not the first prophets, but their period marks the coming of age of the prophetic role. In the Old Testament, a prophet was a person who had unusual gifts and insight. Several attributes marked a prophet.

A prophet stated plainly that he believed he had divine authority. He would say, "Thus saith the Lord;" then he would say what the Lord had to say. We are often suspicious of people who come out with such statements. I have serious questions about the emotional stability of some of the people I hear regularly declaring that the Lord has told them something. The biblical conviction was that if a person made such a statement, the events must ultimately justify that authority.

The expectation regarding the judging of a prophet's integrity is set out in Deuteronomy. Two conditions are clearly set forth.

If a prophet appears and shows some supernatural power, he still must be checked out. "If a prophet or one who foretells dreams appears among you and announces to you a miraculous sign or wonder, and if the sign or wonder of which he has spoken takes place, and he says, 'Let us follow other gods' . . . you must not listen to the words of that prophet or dreamer." (Deuteronomy 13:1-3)

In other words, the Old Testament anticipated that individuals would appear, claiming—and indeed exercising—supernatural powers. Those facts, in themselves, would not be enough to confirm that these people came from God. A test of that would be whether they encouraged the worship of the God of the Bible—or tried to discourage such worship. Fidelity to Jehovah was always the first standard to judge the authenticity of the prophet.

The same book, Deuteronomy, sets out another important criterion. In it, the Lord promises that he will send Israel a prophet who will speak for them.

The people's anxieties about reality are verbalized as follows, "You may say to yourselves, 'How can we know when a message has not been spoken by the Lord?' " The response comes back: "If what a prophet proclaims in the name of the Lord does not take place or come true, that is a message the Lord has not spoken. That prophet has spoken presumptuously. Do not be afraid of him" (Deuteronomy 18:21,22).

In other words, a prophet who speaks about the future and turns out to be wrong or inaccurate is, by that event, confirmed not to be a prophet of the Lord. Not many modern prophets, inside or outside the church, would survive those criteria.

The Bible also defines a prophet as one who is prepared to rebuke sin and evil. It mattered not to the prophet the particular status of the person needing the rebuke. The conspicuous example of that type of rebuke occurred when Nathan confronted David for the murder of Uriah and his adultery with Uriah's wife, Bathsheba (2 Samuel 12).

A prophet clearly was a person touched by the Spirit. When the Spirit of the Lord came on prophets, they spoke—not simply from their own imagination, ideas or efforts, but out of the touching of the Spirit.

They were outspoken people who were not afraid to tackle the power structures or the social injustice of their day. They would declare what God did not approve of and promise God's punishment. A prophet would passionately declare, "Let judgement roll down like waters and righteousness like a mighty stream." Judgement, in this case, was to fall on Israel, not just its pagan neighbors.

A prophet was also a person who could forecast the future. It was not his primary function, but was one of them. Some "experts" claim to be able to forecast the future today. Jean Dixon is one such person. When we read her forecasts, however, we find she is wrong as often as she is right. When she is right, it is by chance, not by insight.

A prophet always spoke out of a sense of constraint. He felt that what he had to say was not simply his responsibility but was God's—and that he spoke only as God's servant. He spoke out of that clear conviction.

Those, then, were the characteristics of a prophet as depicted in the Old Testament. Elijah was the first such prophet and Elisha succeeded him. Both belonged to a wealthy farming family and were recognized in the community as godly men. Both were possessed of unusual powers from God. The books of the Kings describe those powers at work within them. One familiar example was that of Naaman, the servant of a Syrian king, who wanted to be healed of his leprosy. It was through Elijah that God healed him, in a remarkable way which, in itself is another story.

The standards by which the Old Testament judged and assessed prophets cannot be any lower today. Not many people meet the criteria.

Having outlined this background with respect to prophets, let me also respond briefly to those who have difficulty accepting Bible miracles, particularly those in the Old Testament. While I sympathize with those who wrestle with such issues, I would acknowledge that I have much more difficulty with believers in a God who never acts like God than I have with the occasional supernatural event. A God who never behaves supernaturally would be a strange God indeed.

Now, let's return to our passage. The incident here was not unlike what has been going on for centuries in the Middle East. If the Syrians were hungry and lazy, they found it much easier to raid the Israelites and steal their crops than to grow their own.

Ethnic and racial hatred gave them an excuse—even as it often does today.

The setting for this story was that Syria's king was attempting to catch up with the king of Israel to punish him, but was consistently finding that someone else got to him first. Eventually, the king of Syria investigated and found that Elisha was the one who "got there first." So he sent his troops to Dothan, with the result that Elisha's servant sustained the terror we referred to earlier.

The servant had forgotten all about the God who had been so good in the past, in the panic of his immediate situation. The immediate conflict and the anxiety it created drove everything else out of his head.

That is easy to do. It is what I call the stubbed-toe view of life.

You know what it is like to wake up at night and climb out of bed to go to the bathroom. On the way there, and, in the dark, you stub your toe.

Now, when I do that, I lose my sense of proportion! In that moment of extreme agony, I think nothing else is more important than my pain. I forget I am not going to die, that the rest of my body is perfectly healthy. I forget I have a wife who loves me—though I don't deserve it.

I lose all sense of everything except my immediate pain. Elisha's servant had that stubbed-toe viewpoint.

Elisha immediately prayed, "Open his eyes that he may see." When God responded to that prayer, the result was that the servant saw the hills of horses and chariots of fire surrounding and protecting Elisha.

Elisha was God's servant; that was his protection. That is all the protection we need, as individual servants of Christ and as a church.

Elisha knew that bad times would come, but he knew the Lord would be there also. He did not ignore reality, but he saw beyond it.

Could it be that God wants to say to you, as you face difficulties, "Yes, you have difficulties. No, I don't want you to pretend that you don't. But I want to stretch your faith beyond them."

We need, in those circumstances, to pray, "Lord, help me to see beyond the immediate." There is little danger that he will ignore our circumstances. There is a greater danger, however, that we will fail to realize that the Lord our God in the midst of us is mighty.

In ignoring the reality of a mighty God, we may well leave a legacy of recognizing the problems but never solving them in His power. In those circumstances, God becomes a figure of history and not of personal reality.

There was obviously a crucial difference between Elisha and his servant. What was it?

Were they different with respect to their godliness, their gifts or their imagination? Perhaps, but none of those was the key difference to which I refer.

The real difference was that Elisha had spiritual insights lacking in his servant.

Why be like Elisha's servant when we can be like Elisha?

How can we be more like Elisha? How can we be freed from a problem-oriented mindset that does not see beyond the obstacle?

Here are a few suggestions.

1. Read the biographies of Christians who saw beyond the immediate and had faith. Doing so helps you to see how God

dealt with real people in real conflict.

2. Go for a quiet walk and lift up your heart to God.

3. Become sensitive to the Spirit; begin listening with "a third ear." Move beyond the sights and sounds and begin to try to hear what the Spirit is saying. Your prayer might well be, "Lord, what would you have me see in these circumstances?"

4. Claim God's promises for yourself. Remember the scriptures which declare "I can do all things through Christ who strengthens me. . . . My God shall supply all your needs according to his riches in glory by Christ Jesus." As you claim such promises, you begin to pray, "Lord, open my spiritual eyes that I may see. Open them that your power and your greatness are more than I perceive."

What was Elisha's servant to see?

He was to see the protection of the Lord. He was to learn that, in the end, no evil will befall God's children. He was to see that the powers of darkness are limited and do not triumph. He was to note that every child of God can rely on his love and faithfulness. He was to see beyond the visible.

There are times in life when external events close in on us like the Syrian army. There seems to be no way out. We forget all our past experience in the panic and fear which devours us.

A friend of mine had a job he very much enjoyed. It was a senior position in a well-known company. He was aware that the company was "down-sizing"—that is, reducing its operation. He knew that his job was threatened.

My friend prayed about it. In his prayers, he told the Lord that he would accept whatever the consequences would be.

Then the worst happened. He was called into the president's office and told he was through.

In spite of what he had anticipated, the reality was devastating to him. Regardless of what he had told the Lord, the termination hit him like a thunderbolt.

Like Elisha's servant, he saw only the armies of Syria.

Understandable? Yes.

Fortunately, my friend did not allow himself to remain in this state of emotional shock. He began, instead, to remind himself of the Lord's continued faithfulness.

He began to see beyond the bleakness of his lost job.

A lost job in our kind of economy is a personal tragedy. It may change your whole life and many of your values. But the employer never has the last word if you are a believer. Let me illustrate once more.

A woman had what she believed was a good marriage. She and her husband had their struggles, but who doesn't? They had children who were now beginning to function independently. They appeared to be entering a tranquil period in their lives. Without any previous warning, however, her husband told her in undebatable words that it was all over between them.

A solid marriage, a shared faith, an apparently warm relationship—without any opportunity for discussion or counsel—was gone.

The woman began to peer down the road to the rest of her life. It looked bleak. Her social life was in ruins, her children were independent and her financial situation was in jeopardy. The armies of Syria had closed in.

She began to try seeing beyond the disaster. She asked the Lord, "What can you do for me, in me and through me?"

She wonderfully and courageously began to rebuild her life. She discovered that the apparent catastrophe did not have the last word; the Lord did. She discovered a vital ministry to people faced with similar devastation.

There is much more to say about the former job and former husband. But above all, this needs to be said: the darkness will not overcome God's children. The Lord is there, strong to care for his children and to see them through.

Both the man who lost his job and the woman who lost her husband faced life-changing circumstances; that cannot be denied. They could have fallen into bitterness, disillusionment and despair. Who could blame them?

When they began to see beyond the catastrophe, however, they discovered resources in the Lord which were far beyond human expectations.

This passage is not asking that you deny the external conflict; it is pleading with you to start to see beyond it.

Will you—can you—begin to do that?

It is too easy to see the darkness, believe the worst and let our lives be ruled by anxiety and fearfulness. We need to ask the

Lord to open our eyes to see his majesty and his faithfulness. He knows the end from the beginning. He knows what conflict is all about, and he responds by asking us, "Is there anything too hard for the Lord?"

Will you let Him minister to you, and then through you?

The words of this worship chorus help us to focus on what he wants us to see:

> Father God, I give all thanks and praise to Thee.
> Father God, my hands I humbly raise to Thee.
> For your power amazes me, amazes me,
> And I stand in awe and worship Father God.

That is an act of worship. To know such a God is a fitting response in a world as difficult as ours.

EXPECTING GOD TO PRODUCE: WILL HE?

II Kings 20:1-11

Before Isaiah had left the middle court, the word of the Lord came to him: "Go back and tell Hezekiah, the leader of my people, 'This is what the Lord, the God of your father David, says: I have heard your prayer and have seen your tears; I will heal you. On the third day from now you will go up to the temple of the Lord. I will add fifteen years to your life. And I will deliver you and this city from the hand of the king of Assyria. I will defend this city for my sake and for the sake of my servant David.' " (II Kings 20:4-6).

My friend went to the doctor's office for a routine examination. The day was sunny and bright; my friend's personal circumstances were more than satisfactory. The only question being considered was, "Why waste a lovely day like this going to the doctor?"

The day did not end the pleasant way in which it had begun. The results of some tests had been returned to the doctor and he had the miserable task of telling my friend that he was terminally ill. There was nothing modern medicine could do except to make the few months left as bearable as possible.

My friend left the doctor's office devastated. "Where is God in all of this?" he asked himself.

He believed in God. He knew the power of prayer. He had many Christian friends and belonged to a church which believed God could and did heal. He was convinced that the last word was with God, not the doctor.

He cried to God for healing.

It is important to affirm my friend in this, but the reality is that he died.

47

Some Christians would argue that he died because of a lack of faith. True, faith does play a part in healing. The absence or presence of faith, however, is not the sole factor in whether a healing takes place. To make it a key factor is to go beyond what the Bible teaches and, in fact, gives short shrift to the idea of the sovereignty of God. If my faith determines the outcome of my illness, then it is not God who determines it.

Nevertheless, my friend, insofar as those close to him are aware, never wavered from his faith. He bore his suffering courageously. He shared his faith in Christ warmly and effectively. When death came, he accepted it.

What would have glorified God most as he faced such a conflict? We hoped, prayed and longed for a miraculous healing. It would have been a spectacular event.

In the long run, however, would it have brought more glory to God than my friend's death, courageously borne?

I do not know the answer to that question. I do know, however, that it is not an irrelevant question. In the particular biblical incident we are looking at, there is considerable evidence that prolonging Hezekiah's life did not glorify God.

We often believe that conflict is what is happening outside of us. We define it as "what people are doing to me."

"Why are they doing that?" we ask.

Or we suggest that "if only so-and-so was different" there would be no conflict.

That is one way of understanding conflict. The conflict which causes the most trouble with me, however, is not what is happening outside of me, but inside. It is not inter-personal, but intra-personal. It is not what others are doing to me but what I am doing, what takes places inside my head and my heart when conflict is present.

To put it another way, the point to consider is how I process the conflict. That is more important than what is happening elsewhere. I have the freedom to react to conflict as I wish. I do not always use that freedom constructively.

In this particular case, Hezekiah's conflict was both external and internal—but primarily internal. He was confronting the prospect of his own death. Such a confrontation is unquestionably one fraught with conflict. How could it be otherwise?

Who would blame Hezekiah for his reaction, on learning that he was to die? He had already talked to Isaiah, the prophet, about his illness. Isaiah's response had been blunt to the point of being unfeeling. "This is what the Lord says, 'Put your house in order because you will die; you will not recover'."

There certainly appeared to be little room to maneuver or negotiate! Very few human beings can absorb the information about their impending death without some kind of emotional storm.

When a person contemplates his or her own death, several emotional reactions set in—so the experts tell us. Our observations, if not our experiences, confirm that.

The first may be denial. "This is not happening to me. I know the doctor says it is but that's not true. I just cannot believe it."

From denial, the next step may be anger. A few years ago, I recall lying down after eating, and beginning to feel pains in my chest and hands. I assumed I was having a heart attack and became quickly persuaded within myself that I was about to die.

In this case, the pain was so extreme that denial quickly turned to anger. During that angry frame of mind one of my children came into the room. She was obviously anxious about what was happening to her father. I remember becoming angry with the child. I contemplated later how my child would have felt if I had died and her last memory of me had been my anger. The anger was my reaction to the possibility of immediate death, not annoyance at my child, but I doubt whether that would have been understood.

We fall into this kind of pattern rapidly when we are so threatened.

From anger, the next step usually is bargaining, followed by depression, then either resignation or acceptance.

Notably, the way in which we handle this kind of process depends to a large extent on our level of Christian belief or lack of it. I am told that if you are either a confirmed atheist or a committed Christian, you can handle the prospect of your death quite well. If you are somewhere in between, the tensions and conflicts begin to move in.

Almost every person will go through the cycle—denial,

anger, bargaining, depression and acceptance. My faith's role is to help me cope with each of the steps, to get me through them and teach me how to accept what is happening. None of these steps occur exactly as described. At times, when you have already moved to another level, you may backtrack.

When Hezekiah faced the prospect of death, he moved rapidly from denial to anger to bargaining. The text notes, "He turned his face to the wall and prayed to the Lord, 'Remember, O Lord, I have walked with you faithfully and wholeheartedly and have done what is good in your eyes.' " Not all of us could make this claim or even be inside the ball park. Hezekiah could.

He did not stop there. The passage tells us, "Hezekiah wept bitterly." It was not just that he squeezed out a tear or two. His weeping was intense, broken, loud and tempestuous.

It is important to note some things about this man Hezekiah. He was not a nominally godly person who cultivated his faith only at a time of emergency. Would you be able to make the kind of claim he did?

He was a good and remarkable man, about whom Scripture says "Hezekiah trusted in the Lord of Israel. There was no one like him among all the kings of Judah, either before him or after him." Considering that the list includes David, Solomon, Josiah and others, that is quite a statement!

Hezekiah's faith and circumstances were tried in the furnace of life. For example, he faced Sennacherib and the Assyrians—described as being like locusts. The Assyrians came into a country and stripped the people of their possessions. They took the best qualified and most able people back to their own land, to work as slaves. They left the country they invaded with no money, no resources, no reserves and no skilled men. During that particular period, they were the nastiest and meanest of all the conquerors. He was the Ghangis Khan of his day.

You may remember the poet Byron wrote:

The Assyrian came down like a wolf to the fold
And his cohorts were gleaming with purple and gold
And the sheen of their spears were like stars in the sea
When the blue waves roll nightly on Lake Galilee.

Poetry is nice but the reality was far from the imagery. Sennacherib had perfected the techniques of violence and intimidation. In II Kings 18, we learn how he beseiged Jerusalem and mocked Hezekiah by declaring, "I will give you 2,000 horses if you can find riders to put on them." His underlings added insult to injury by shouting messages in Hebrew directly to the beseiged residents of Jerusalem, bypassing their leaders. Psychological warfare is not a modern invention.

A wonderful deliverance of Jerusalem was effected, ultimately, and Sennacherib failed in his attempted conquest. In the process, nevertheless, Hezekiah's faith was tried in the furnace of life and his godliness emerged. He believed in the sovereignty of God and demonstrated his concern, not simply for his own survival but for God's glory.

Hezekiah was therefore a good and capable man facing death. Why did he have difficulty with that prospect?

For that matter, why do we have trouble facing death? And what part does faith play in changing that?

In the first place, Hezekiah found it hard to face death simply because he was human. The fear of death is universal. I sometimes wonder whether God gave us the fear of death to protect us from self-destruction.

It is fascinating to observe how different people contemplate death.

Speaking as a secularist, Bertrand Russell said there was darkness without and "when I die, there will be darkness within. There is no splendor, only the triviality of the moment, then nothing."

A non-Christian mystic wrote, "Death is at my door. He has crossed the unknown sea and brought this call to my home. The night is dark and my heart is fearful. Yet I will take up the lamp, open my gates and bow to him my welcome."

He saw beyond where Bertrand Russell was at. Even though the thought of death made him anxious, he believed there was something beyond—and welcomed it.

Another great secular name of this century, Camus, notes, "I do not want to believe that death is the gateway to another life. For me, it is a closed door." It is interesting the way Camus phrases it: "I do not want to believe." In other words, his unbelief does not grow out of an intellectual conviction so much as out of desire.

The prospect of death triggers the human feeling that "it should not be coming for me." Further, it stems from the fear of the unknown. The Bible does not condemn us for either the resistance or the fear.

It is possible to defend Hezekiah in his reaction to his impending death, in part because the revelation Jesus Christ has given us was not yet in place. Hezekiah did not know Him who is the resurrection and the life. He did not know the one who said, "Whosoever liveth and believeth in me shall never die." and "I go to prepare a place for you. And if I go, I will come again and receive you unto myself, that where I am, there ye may be also."

He did not know Christ.

It would have made a difference if he had, but he still would have faced the human predicament of being temporarily overwhelmed. There is no need to put him down spiritually because of his reaction.

It was not only that Hezekiah was reacting as a normal human being, to the reality of his imminent death. He could have been saying, "I have things to do, Lord. Don't you know that? How could you come for me now?"

If you have walked through Jerusalem, as I have, you will be aware of one of the things he wanted to complete. It was a tunnel bringing water from its supply sources right into the heart of the city, inside its walls. It brought a much greater sense of security to that city, which, until then, had no internal water supply. Its residents could now more easily survive a seige.

Have you, like Hezekiah, said, "Lord, I have my agenda and your agenda does not fit into mine. Won't you change your mind? There are things left undone that I need to do, Lord. Give me more time."?

Hezekiah was not ready to go. Are we ever ready?

What we do learn from this passage is that Hezekiah believed it was quite legitimate to place demands on God. When God tells him to put his house in order because he is going to die, he turns his face to the wall and says to God, "Remember, O Lord, how I walked before you faithfully, with wholehearted devotion and have done what is good in your eyes." And he weeps bitterly.

He is reminding God of his faithful service and on that basis pleads for an extended lifespan.

I want to affirm that making demands on God is a legitimate activity. This is true even when we do not have as adequate a basis for bargaining as did Hezekiah. There is a fine line, however, between pleading our case with God and expecting God to produce.

This passage affirms that it is an act of faith in God to make demands of Him. It is confirmed elsewhere in scripture. In II Corinthians 12, Paul does it. Jesus did it with the Father in the Garden of Gethsemane. If you have not made demands on God, perhaps your faith—or your perception of God—is too small. Indeed, His grace and His power are such that none can ever ask too much. The Bible asks rhetorically, "Is anything too hard for God?"

But was Hezekiah right in this case? It so happens that he gained what he demanded: 15 extra years. However, two disastrous things befell him during that time.

One was that the King of Babylon's ambassador was invited to inspect Hezekiah's treasure. The prophet was disgusted with Hezekiah and informed him that the King of Babylon would come back later and collect. After Hezekiah died, he did just that.

The second was that Manasseh was born. He was as disastrous as Hezekiah was godly. Manasseh was 12 years old when Hezekiah eventually died, and he reigned for 55 years. When Manasseh was finished, so was Jerusalem.

Hezekiah was certainly a good, upright and godly man who had been tried in the furnace of life. He bargained with God and, in the process, both won and lost.

He makes us face the dilemma which admits that, while I have the right to demand of God, I need to remember that getting what I want out of God is not necessarily the good news I think it is.

Does God, in these situations, take advantage of my vulnerability? Is it fair that He would give me something I want, which later turns sour or bitter? How do I know when to back off?

There are so many questions here, to which there are no easy answers. I do not believe that God just plays with us when we are in conflict as ultimate as the one Hezekiah faced. But I do know that to have had his life extended as he did was not the triumphant experience he would have wanted.

Most of us would respond positively to the prospect of having one's life prolonged. A spectacular healing is a very special happening. All I am pleading for is the realization that there are other ways in which God may be glorified. To face death with faith and courage is sometimes an even greater spiritual triumph.

The bottom line question is always, "Am I willing for God to glorify Himself by life or by death?"

The crucial way of dealing with the internal conflict that such a possibility raises is to accept that the process of denial, anger, bargaining, depression and acceptance is natural and normal. None of it is a denial of our faith and trust in the Lord.

He will see me through all of these steps. All through it I need to ask him, "How can I glorify you?"

It will not always be easy to ask that question—or to hear God's response. I do not want to criticize Hezekiah, but I do want to understand what this passage is saying.

The heart of the answer to those questions could lie with the part of Hezekiah's prayer on a previous occasion, when he told God, "You alone are God over all the kings of the earth." If we are in the "Hezekiah predicament" we may well learn to say, "Lord, this is what I need and want. I know you can deliver and I know I will be very disappointed if you don't.

"But I want you to know that I accept your will for my life."

At times, there wells up within us a need for God to do what we want Him to—and what we know would be so apparently easy for Him to accomplish. At those times, it is legitimate to "lay it on the line" with God, to say, "I believe I know what is best for me right now, but I am willing for you to make the final choice."

Why is it so difficult to take that extra step? It may be that we cannot cope with the circumstances of the moment. It is true, too, that justice does not always prevail, that some people have a harder time and deeper struggles than others. For some, their emotions in life are more complicated and their experiences are more difficult.

Is it that some people have a stronger, simpler faith than others? As I read about Hezekiah, I note that he had a simple and profound faith, yet he found himself in this predicament.

Sometimes, one simply has to say, "Lord, here are my circumstances. They are creating havoc. I do not know where to turn. I want you to change my circumstances but I am willing for you to be Lord."

What a step of faith!

But what a reward there is in the future. No matter what God's answer is, acceptable or unacceptable, pleasant or unpleasant, palatable or unpalatable, I will trust and not be afraid.

That challenge was there for Hezekiah and it is there for you and me today.

PRAISING GOD BEFORE HE ACTS

II Chronicles 20:1-17

O our God, did you not drive out the inhabitants of this land before your people Israel and give it forever to the descendents of Abraham your friend? They have lived in it and have built in it a sanctuary for your name, saying, 'If calamity comes upon us, whether the sword of judgement or plague or famine, we will stand in your presence before this temple that bears your Name and will cry out to you in our distress, and you will hear us and save us.' (II Chronicles 20:7-9)

Recently, I read the autobiography of Abba Eban, the brilliant Israeli foreign minister. In it, he recounts the part he has played in Israel's emergence. His involvement dates to his student days at Cambridge. At that time, and on a number of occasions, all seemed lost. The British government, with Ernest Bevin as foreign secretary, was determined to make no concessions as Israel struggled for nationhood and recognition after World War II.

At other times, the Russians appeared ready either to make war on Israel directly, or to plunge the world into the final conflict—or even both.

In the Yom Kippur War, the Israelis were caught unprepared and came close to being wiped out.

The interesting point about all this was that several times, Eban says in effect, that all that was left for him and his colleagues to do was pray. The impression he communicates is that of a man who did not much believe in prayer, except as a last resort. It was certainly not a priority in his personal life, as he tells it. Nor was it a means of seeking God's guidance before acting. It was something to fall back on when nothing else could be attempted.

The chapter we are looking at records an older crisis faced by Israel. Their neighbors—Moab, Amman and others—had assembled "a vast army." Jehoshaphat was the king of Judah at the time. He vacillated between his political judgement and his desire to put God first. Too often, his "practical" wisdom won out.

Are you like Jehoshaphat in that way? Does practical wisdom seem more attractive to you than God's wisdom?

Jehoshaphat had made an alliance with Ahab, king of Israel. That alliance made all kinds of political sense but had no spiritual integrity. He was warned against it by the prophets, but chose to ignore the warning. In the battle with their neighbors, Ahab was killed and Jehoshaphat escaped.

When Jehoshaphat returned to Jerusalem, the prophet Jehu met him and directed some forthright words at him. "Should you help the wicked and love those who hate the Lord? Because of this, the wrath of God is upon you. There is, however, some good in you, for you have rid the land of the Asherah poles and have set your heart in seeking God (II Chronicles 19:2,3).

It seems that Jehoshaphat took this to heart and set about serving God in a more whole-hearted fashion.

I would encourage you to be like Jehoshaphat in that respect. It certainly paid off for him. That was hardly an adequate motive for his actions. Nevertheless, it was the result of a right decision.

This brings us to the crisis and conflict to which this particular biblical passage refers. In this crisis, Jehoshaphat reacted differently—and more desirably—than he had when he was relying on political judgement. On this occasion, he "resolved to enquire of the Lord and he proclaimed a fast for all Judah." No longer did he view seeking the Lord as some kind of last resort. He saw it as the first thing to do. It is interesting to note, too, that he called on the people to fast along with him.

In Protestant churches, there is a revival of interest in fasting. Richard Foster's *Celebration of Discipline* outlines some procedures and cautions. The purpose of fasting in this biblical setting was to indicate to God the seriousness with which the people were approaching Him. It was also a conscious act of self-denial. That it may or may not have had particular side benefits for one's health or weight is purely coincidental.

Both individuals and churches are, in our day, beginning to rediscover the spiritual power of prayer and fasting. Certainly Jehoshaphat did on this occasion.

In every phrase one can sense the intensity with which Jehoshaphat approached the Lord. There were no strings of pious platitudes or repetitious phrases. The circumstances were too fearful and the God he sought, too awesome.

It is important to notice exactly how this troubled man appealed to the Lord. It forms a model for us when we are in the middle of crisis and conflict.

Jehoshaphat placed his full reliance and hope in the character, promises and power of God. He says, "O Lord, God of our Fathers, are you not the God who is in heaven?"

He continues by reviewing the long-term relationships between God and the Israelites. He reminds God of what He has done in the past: delivering them from their enemies, giving them the land and accepting the sanctuary built to honor and glorify Him.

Having completed that process, he reviews the promise God had made. The implication was that there was more involved than his and his people's right to call on God when calamity struck. There was also the necessity for them to be in a right relationship with God. This clearly inferred repentance for spiritual failure.

It is not enough to lay demands on God for Him to act. There is an imperative on our part to so live and act that God will hear our prayer.

There was always a spiritual dimension involved in the issue of defeat or victory, when it came to the facing of enemies.

Richard Lovelace in *The Dynamics of Spiritual Life* (IVP) points out the cycle of spiritual failure and recovery that typified the history of these people. The decline began with the emergence of a new generation who had not experienced first hand what God had done. Their spiritual indifference led them to abandon their sole allegiance to Jehovah; they began to adopt the culture and religious affiliation of their neighbors. The consequence was a calamity for the nation. The calamity could take the form of famine, plague or defeat in war. The cure was always repentance, genuine prayer and spiritual reform. Out of this, their fortunes were restored, though almost as soon as everything settled down, the cycle began again.

To change the metaphor, they kept going around the same ball park. Lovelace argues that central to the spiritual renewal, which led to economic and political benefits, was always a charismatic leader. He sees the pattern in the book of Judges as classic. Here, with Jehoshaphat, we have a charismatic leader who has worked through his ambivalence and was, at this point, fully committed to the Lord.

When he realized the circumstances which confronted him, Jehoshaphat did not attempt to hide the realities from himself or his people. "We have no power to face this vast army that is attacking us." The situation was beyond him. "We do not know what to do, but our eyes are upon you." He did not minimize, rationalize or deny.

The fact that it would have done him no good to have minimized, rationalized or denied does not alter the truth. It is too easy to slip into that kind of attitude. Even if our enemies are less obvious and have to do with internal as well as with external forces, they need to be seen with the clear eyes of a Jehoshaphat.

Like Jehoshaphat, you would find it useful to identify those enemies that encircle your life. Insecurity, lack of personal worth, disillusionment, despair, wilful sin, unresolved conflict—they can run the range from simple failure to love others to deliberate rebellion against the clear teaching of the Bible.

Jehoshaphat came to the place where he knew his own powerlessness. He had difficulty reaching that point, but, eventually, he did. The lesson of the humiliating defeat with Ahab had sunk in.

Why is it so difficult for us to admit the obvious in our lives? It is liberating to acknowledge that only the Lord can help me. When I do that, it is always the very beginning of victory. It is never a source of humiliation.

The pressure and conflict Jehoshaphat found, once again,

appeared to be external. The real battle, however, had to be fought within him, before the victory could be won. He then emerged as what Lovelace describes as the kind of charismatic leader who was capable of taking his people to victory. In spiritual warfare, "we have no power" in ourselves. We do have unlimited resources in the Lord.

Once again, it is to be noted the issue is not what is happening outside myself but what is happening inside. It is how, and with whom, it is processed.

How then, did God respond to Jehoshaphat's prayer?

Perhaps it should be pointed out that God was responding to Jehoshaphat as the representative of the community, not simply as an individual. This point is emphasized repeatedly in II Chronicles 20. For example verse 5 says, "They came from every town in Judah to seek Him."

When the people began to take God seriously, He began to respond to them. "The battle is not yours, but the Lord's" (verse 20). The conviction is clear all through Scripture, that when God's people turn in passionate sincerity to Him, He blesses them.

God responded with a clear, unequivocal message, delivered through a man named Jahaziel (verse 14). In the inner heart of Jahaziel, the Lord gave a message for His people.

That message was one of reassurance and encouragement. "Do not be afraid or discouraged," was the expression used to begin and conclude the word from the Lord. His point was summarized in these words: "You will not have to fight this battle. Take up your positions, stand firm and see the deliverance the Lord will give you" (verse 17).

What a special word from the Lord! It so exactly fitted their need. It was such good news that they must have had some difficulty believing it, although the passage does not suggest that. Indeed, not a cynical voice was heard. Nobody said, "Let us wait and see." The immediate reaction was to burst out into worship and praise.

It is interesting to note, as well, the fact that worship and praise became central to the whole encounter. Verse 10 tells us that Jehoshaphat bowed his face to the ground and all the people of Judah and Jerusalem fell down and worshiped before the

Lord. The Levites and their allies stood and praised the Lord *with a loud voice.*

I might gently suggest that sometimes our praise is so quiet—especially in traditional churches—that if God was not a supernatural being, He would not be able to hear it. The absence of worship, adoration and praise impoverishes our lives and even our churchgoing.

In verse 21, we are told that Jehoshaphat appointed a group of men to sing to the Lord and to praise him for the splendor of his holiness. The important point to note here is that the praise was both spontaneous and organized. Further, the praise began before the battle began, before the victory was won.

Indeed, praise, in some ways, is both the most surprising and the most significant element in this whole incident.

Not only that, but God used the praise itself as a means to the victory.

They began to praise the Lord in anticipation of the victory he promised. They did not even wait for the battle to be joined. Their faith and convictions were assured.

Too many of us forget to praise God after we have won a victory. Like Abba Eban, we put it down to unusual circumstances, our own skill or coincidence. These people started their praise before they achieved victory because they knew the One who would give them that victory.

Their action, in itself, was a victory—as well as a key to the victory in battle. When we begin to have the confidence in the Lord which enables us to praise Him, it opens up the road to victory. It is an act of vibrant faith. It is not something passive. It is not a modest hope that maybe God will do something, or a vague feeling that something will turn up to change the dreaded and anticipated result. It is a positive conviction that God has spoken and that He will do what he has promised.

HOW DID JESUS
HANDLE CONFLICT?

Matthew 26:36-46

Going a little farther, he fell with his face to the ground and
prayed, "My Father, if it is possible, may this cup be taken from
me. Yet not as I will, but as you will." (Matthew 26:39)

This passage is one of the most emotionally difficult in the
whole Bible, because it is the story of our Lord's conflict in the
Garden of Gethsemane.

In previous chapters, we have been looking at the issue of
conflict, utilizing issues in the lives of Rehoboam, Elisha and
others as points of reference. We have worked from the Old
Testament books of I Kings, II Kings and II Chronicles. We
conclude our consideration of the biblical ways of handling conflict by seeing how Jesus himself acted.

Did he experience conflict, too? How did he cope with it?
How relevant is it to our lives, anyway?

All these questions are legitimate. Obviously, I believe
Jesus experienced real conflict. Clearly, he coped with it effectively. If I did not think it relevant, it would hardly be
worthwhile considering it.

But, before we look more directly into Jesus' handling of
conflict, let me set up some fairly typical human conflicts,
similar to the kinds many of us face in our lives.

The first is about a husband and wife who are locked into a
conflict which is important to both of them: a not-unusual, not-
incredible, not-unlikely but normal situation. This couple has
trouble resolving conflict in their marriage at the best of times,
but this is a more serious case.

In this particular conflict, the wife feels torn. She believes, with some justification, that her husband is wrong on the point at issue. She believes he is inconsiderate and about to be financially irresponsible. There is a good deal at stake both for them and their family. Simply put, she finds she cannot get him to communicate with her on the issue. He will not talk about it. She can force the issue but there will be a price to pay. The relationship will sour through his insecurity and immaturity.

What should she do?

There are apparently some alternatives open to her.

Should she be silent and withdraw? Should she take him on with all the risks that involves? Should she pray and leave it with the Lord? Or, should she talk with someone else about the issue?

Her mind runs from one alternative to another. She is dismayed and discouraged.

The second situation involves a young couple who are considering marriage (Nowadays, that is, in itself, encouraging.)

One of the two is a devout Christian; the other is not. The Christian is afraid to raise the issue, because it might end the relationship. So they marry without discussing the difference, let alone resolving it. The Christian hopes and believes that their love for each other will see them through.

After the marriage takes place, they begin to argue heatedly about issues such as money, church attendance, lifestyle, leisure and friends.

As they should have known, all the matters they ignored before marriage have now become sources of tension between them. In addition, the differences in their values and convictions lie at the center of every argument.

How should a Christian in such a marriage deal with that kind of conflict? Should he or she placate the non-Christian, blame him/herself for getting into the relationship or begin to find fault with the other person?

What is the bottom line?

The third involves a person who finds himself in a job in which he is expected to do things which, while being common practice in that business, are unethical—and, indeed, at the least, marginally illegal.

(This, unfortunately, is not unusual today. I talked to a

friend recently who said that when he began the work he was doing some years ago, the job had its "white areas," "grey areas" and "black areas." Nowadays, all the areas are black. The combination of a poor economy and strong competition in his industry has not improved the ethics of the industry.)

The man in our illustration is under pressure to do unethical things. He has been asked to lie, to falsify reports and to participate in kickbacks. He tells himself, "The economy I am living in is bad and a job is a job. What will I do and what will happen to my family if I refuse?"

If he loses the job, the prospects of getting another in the same business are poor. Furthermore, he is likely to find himself in the same conflicts in any new job he gets. No former employer is likely to supply a reference which says, "He left because he was more honorable than we are."

If the man acts unethically, he goes against his conscience; he is disobedient to Christ. He will be troubled by guilt and depression. He could even end up in court on criminal charges.

Conversely, idealism does not pay the bills.

The previous type of situation is not entirely unfamiliar to me. Before becoming a minister, I worked in a builders' suppliers office, during World War II. For two weeks, at one point, I filled in for one of the managers while he was on holiday.

He had given me instructions that I was not to sell a particular item to a certain customer, because the customer was irresponsible.

When that person came in and asked for the item in question, I told more of the truth than I was supposed to. Was I simply naïve? I am sure it could have been handled better. I was more concerned, however, with my convictions than with the manager's anger.

As it happened, the manager attended the church I belonged to. When he learned of my action, he told me, "What you do on Sunday has nothing to do with what you do Monday to Friday." He had difficulty containing his annoyance at my ineptness, as he saw it. (My perception was that I was simply being zealously honest!)

How does one resolve these kinds of conflicts? How does one live with oneself when facing these kinds of conflict? Did

Jesus know anything about this kind of stuff?

Some people believe that Jesus had a very quiet and easy life until about five days before his death. They think he went for long walks with his disciples, cured people who were blind, sick or had leprosy—but never knew much about conflict.

But the opposite is the truth. In fact, when he was born, the word to his mother was that he would be rejected by many in Israel—and this to their undoing.

The truth is that Jesus' life was one long conflict, from the incident with the moneychangers in the temple to the time when religious leaders tried to stone him because he apparently broke the Sabbath and made himself equal with God. At times, he himself sought and induced conflict for what he saw as valid reasons. For example, he took on the Pharisees, offending them considerably by telling them, "You are like beautiful mausoleums, full of dead men's bones, foulness and corruption. You try to look like saintly men but underneath those pious robes of yours are hearts besmirched with every kind of hypocrisy and sin."

If someone said that to me, I believe I would be offended, too, especially if it was true—as, in this case, it was.

His most intensive conflict took place in the garden of Gethsemane.

Immediately before he went to the cross he experienced bitter and humiliating conflict, as well. He was spat on. He was crowned with a crown of thorns. His tormenters blindfolded him, struck him and told him to guess who was doing it.

One of his disciples denied him; another betrayed him. The depth of his turmoil was reflected when he cried out, "My soul is crushed with horror and sadness to the point of death."

This passage in Matthew 26, if anything, underplays the feelings Jesus experienced. There is an agony here which is quite beyond human capacity to grasp.

All the human factors which cause any of us grief were present. Jesus was intensely lonely. That is hard to bear at any time in one's life. It is even more difficult to be lonely and feel deserted when passing through the roughest crisis.

In this passage, Jesus had specifically asked three of his most closely trusted disciples to stay awake and pray for him.

They fell asleep; whether they did so because of emotional exhaustion or indifference to his needs is academic. The reality is that they failed him in his hour of need. They let him be alone. Also involved in this incident was Jesus' contemplation of what lay ahead of him: the rejection by those who, a few days earlier, had acclaimed him.

Again, it can be argued that the cause of their rejection was his failure to live up to their expectations. That was little comfort for him.

His thoughts must have included the physical horror of the crucifixion ordeal. Even in a world as satiated by violence as ours, death on a cross remains deeply repulsive.

There was much more here. Calvin says that Jesus endured "the torments of a condemned and lost sinner." The deepest level of conflict in this event lay in the direct confrontation with Satan—as well as the reality that Jesus himself was bearing our sins.

This spiritual battle, of such monumental importance to God as well as to us, made the conflict pointedly horrendous.

It is vital to note that in this particular case, Jesus longed to be spared the ordeal. "If it be possible," he cried out, "may this cup be taken from me." This was no idle prayer. All the intensity of his being went into it. But the cup could not be avoided. The consequences of this issue were too momentous—for him and for us.

When we are locked into a conflict that cannot be avoided, Jesus, above all people, understands our reaction.

When we go through marital or job conflict—or anything else which threatens—and we talk to Jesus about it, we are talking to someone who has experienced conflict at its deepest possible level. His conflicts, indeed, were beyond our capacity to understand. The New Testament makes it clear that many of our Lord's conflicts were with demonic powers.

Consider Matthew 13:27. It says, "Did you not sow good seed in your fields? Whence hath it tares? An enemy hath done this." And part of the Lord's Prayer notes, "Deliver us from the evil one." In Gethsemane, he says to Simon Peter that "Satan has desired to have you that he may sit you at his feet."

In Luke 22:53, he noted, "This is your hour—when

darkness reigns." In Luke 10, he said, "I beheld Satan fall as lightning from heaven."

All these passages indicate that the Lord's conflict was in the realm of the supernatural. He struggled with powers and forces beyond our human understanding—indeed, outside our frame of reference.

It is fascinating to note that Jesus was not afraid of conflict—except at Gethsemane. He was torn apart, there, not simply by natural anxiety but by the enormity of what was taking place.

It is also important to learn that Jesus dealt with conflict in several ways. Sometimes he withdrew, as on the occasion when he said to his disciples, "Come with me by yourselves to a quiet place and get some rest" (Mark 6:31). (Incidentally, they did not get the rest they desired.)

At other times, he vigorously sought the conflict, as in his verbal jousts with the Pharisees.

And, on some occasions, he legitimately sidestepped potential conflict, by refusing to "rise to the bait" placed by his detractors. Do you remember the time he was asked to whom tribute should be paid? He replied, "Render to Caesar that which is Caesar's and to God that which is God's."

Another approach to conflict practised by Jesus was exploration. In John 4, for example, in talking with the Samaritan woman, he discussed a number of things before confronting her with the real issue.

There was a natural animosity between Jews and Samaritans, which Jesus simply ignored as the conversation began. There was a generally felt cultural uneasiness about the kind of openness he demonstrated in speaking with a woman. There were ethnic, gender and ethical—and religious—differences to be faced. All these, then as now, were dynamite to deal with.

Yet Jesus built bridges with the woman. He explored those differences, treated her virtually as an equal, yet did not ignore the barriers. It was only after carefully exploring the differences that he put his finger on her broken marital relationships.

In dealing with Nicodemus, the Pharisee who came to him by night, Jesus levelled with him quickly, by declaring, "You must be born again."

The contrast between his abruptness with Nicodemus and his comparative gentleness with the Samaritan woman is instructive. If he had been as short with her, he would have terminated the relationship before it began. If he had been overly gentle with Nicodemus, the Pharisee's defenses would not have been penetrated.

Jesus dealt with conflict, therefore, in many ways. It can be safely assumed, however, that Jesus loved people, even when they created conflict for him and with him.

Whether he used withdrawal, evasion, exploration or leveling—or fought the issue to the death, Jesus always tried to keep the door open. When the door was closed, it was not Jesus who closed it.

Consider, for example, the parable of the prodigal son—and the elder brother. When Jesus told it to the Pharisees, it was a parable of invitation. To them, he said, in effect, "You are like the elder brother. I understand why you feel angry, but come on in. There is a celebration and there is room for you."

Even with the Pharisees, then, he kept the door open until they slammed it closed, locked it and barred it—and destroyed themselves.

In evaluating how Jesus dealt with conflict, however, it is important to note the results he achieved as well as the methods he chose.

In the four scenarios we sketched at the beginning of this chapter, the consistent question was, "What is the bottom line?"

It is fascinating to note that Jesus' bottom line is very different from yours and mine. My bottom line was, "Can I be a Christian and keep my job?" For another person it was, "Can I hold my marriage together?" Still others might ask, "What is to my advantage in the circumstances?" or "How can I deal with this overwhelming anxiety?"

Too often, our bottom line is an attempt to assess how little damage we can cause ourselves.

The bottom line, for some, goes further than mere self-interest. It reads, "I will show them who is toughest." John Mitchell, Richard Nixon's attorney-general, was a tragic illustration of that kind of bottom line. He lived by the adage, "When the going gets tough, the tough get going." He ended up with a broken marriage, a dead wife, a term in jail and a reputation in tatters.

Another bottom line causes me to grit my teeth and declare that I will have my way on a particular issue. No matter what the consequences, I will get what I want.

Do you respond in any of these ways?

For Jesus, however, the bottom line was simple, *"How can I fulfill the purpose of God? How can I glorify him?"*

With Jesus, of course, there were short-term ways of dealing with the long-term bottom line. Those short terms came in personal encounters, as with the Samaritan woman at the well. The long term involved the cross and the resurrection. Luke 9:51 tells us that Jesus resolutely set out for Jerusalem. He knew Jerusalem would mean Gethsemane, denial, betrayal, the cry of dereliction and his death on the cross. He also knew it meant resurrection and he set that as his bottom line.

Jesus showed clear singlemindedness in dealing with conflict. It was a singlemindedness, not of process, but regarding his goal.

Some of our conflict comes because we want to have our cake and eat it, too. We want to be inside the Christian ball park, but not to follow Christ where it costs.

We find that conflict gets mixed up with personality issues: how we act and how we perceive the actions of other people. Some people like to withdraw. Others like to fight or dominate. Some are natural decision-makers.

The questions surrounding the way we handle conflict are complicated. Each person seems to fall into a particular style. That style becomes the focal point, rather than the settling of the real issues in conflict.

The real issue, however, is not just how we cope with the conflict but what happens in the end. Some people never reach that end point. The questions to be asked relate to the importance of the relationship. We need to ask, "How can I glorify God in this situation?"

That is your bottom line. While other issues like getting what one wants, personal growth and achieving a "proper fit" need to be considered, the ultimate matter for the Christian is the Lordship of Christ.

In the kinds of conflict illustrated at the beginning of this sermon, this is the unavoidable question. In some of the illustrations, the fact that the question about Christ's Lordship was not asked early enough made the issues unbearably complicated. In others, the answer is not simple or straightforward. In others, still, the answer is hard because it has clear personal complications—like the loss of a job.

No matter what, the Lordship of Christ—the glorifying of God—is the overriding question.

In the short term, that can sometimes be tough. I will wonder whether I can make it. I know what I want and what the Lord wants and they seem to be in conflict.

It is not always easy to hang in there under these pressures, is it?

At times, I know what will make me feel good right now and I realize it is not what the Lord wants me to do. I need to learn to resist the short-term reaction. I will put the Lord first.

Conflict is a normal part of life. If you handle it well, the quality of your life will be special. If you handle it badly, you bring misery on yourself and the people whose lives you touch.

From our Lord's example, it appears there is no one best way to cope with conflict. Sometimes withdrawal will be better than fighting—or vice versa. Or there are other options, depending on certain circumstances.

If you are attempting to manipulate or second-guess someone else, that will end up badly. If you are unaware of your own basic needs, that too will be wrong.

The bottom line is, "Am I willing to put the Lord first?" It assumes that you know the Lord's will. You may need to talk with someone more mature or more objective, to get an accurate reading on that. There is no arguing that the answers are not always easily predictable. It is possible that putting the Lord first may intensify the conflict.

Because the conflict is intensified, you may have a hard time for a while, but in the end, your decision will be life-enhancing and joy-bringing.

A doctor I know was a practising surgeon in one of

Canada's largest hospitals. His specialty was operating on the tongue. (I am sure he had many Christians as his customers!) Only one other surgeon in the province of British Columbia had the same specialty and he was due for retirement. My friend could have cleaned up. His professional and financial future were secure.

But tugging away at him and his wife was their knowledge of the shortage of doctors and nurses in the third world.

Where is he today?

He and his wife live in one of the nations of Africa. He is working in a mission hospital. Have you ever seen those little mission hospitals? They are disorganized and untidy. The smallest Canadian hospital has likely thrown out more equipment than there is in that African facility.

That doctor's bottom line was, "I will put the needs of people in the third world ahead of my own financial and professional future." That approach grew out of his and his wife's commitment to Christ.

I would suggest that, with all his frustrations, he is a happier person than most of the doctors practising in the hospital from which he came. What he has done is life-enhancing and joy-producing.

Jesus has been described as the one "who for the joy that was set before him, endured the cross, despising the shame and is sat down at the right hand of the throne of God."

What is your bottom line?

Any bottom line falling short of serious consideration of the Lordship of Christ brings you only temporary relief. In the long term, however, it simply increases the conflict and robs you of joy.

The biblical way of dealing with conflict is to acknowledge that "What will glorify God?" is, in the end, the only big question worth asking.

It needs to be the question you are asking yourself.

RESOLVING CONFLICT IN THE LOCAL CHURCH

Acts 15:1, 2

Some men came down from Judea and were teaching the brothers: "Unless you are circumcised according to the custom taught by Moses, you cannot be saved." This brought Paul and Barnabas into sharp dispute and debate with them.

I grew up in a little Baptist Church in Northern Ireland where the people nurtured and cared for me spiritually and emotionally. They not only brought me to Christ, but they discipled me in the faith. I will never cease to be grateful for that group of people, who were for me, in many ways, like an extended family.

However, there was a group of people in that church for whom church arguments and conflict were their very meat and drink. The range of activities permitted to them was so restrictive, perhaps, that they needed a place to let off steam. Their safety valve, so to speak, was the church business meeting.

The activities of that particular group have left me with a lifetime of anxiety with respect to church business meetings—an anxiety, thankfully, not often borne out by experience.

The particular subjects for argument both amaze and amuse me as I recall them. At one meeting, a prominent church member itemized and deemed unacceptable certain books in the pastor's library. The pastor defended his right to have whatever books he chose—even books containing points of view different from his own. The result was an animated row over the extent of the minister's freedom to choose his books.

Fortunately, the pastor won, though he was somewhat scarred in the process.

There were heated arguments about the pastor's views on the second coming of Christ. This particular pastor had absorbed some of the traditional Christian views, which happened not to be in conformity with the Scofield Bible.

I vividly recall another argument over whether the pastor should be permitted to attend the Protestant ministerial in that town. Our town was predominantly Presbyterian and the Baptists regarded the Presbyterians—with some justification in that particular instance—as being theologically liberal.

I cannot remember whether the church gave him permission. I do recall, however, that, in the end, he was not invited to join because some of the Presbyterians deemed it inappropriate for a Baptist to be a part of the ministerial. With the general reputation of the church for being contentious, they could hardly be blamed.

The pastor survived the arguments but I have the feeling they did not do his ministry in that church much good. At times, they devastated him.

As I recall those conflicts, based as they were more on personality than theology, I recognize that the attitudes and the resultant divisions in the church were destructive to the church's witness. There had to be a better way of settling the power struggles which were at the heart of these differences.

The church became conspicuous, not for their witness to the truth of the *Good News*, but for their church fights. People in the town could not get by the rows in order to hear what else they had to say. Everyone, as a consequence, lost. The Baptist church lost because it could not reach people who would otherwise have responded. The community lost because it was cut off from this church's witness to the gospel. The behavior of that Baptist church caused me to ask then, as I do now, "Were the people of the New Testament church better at recognizing and resolving conflict?" If they were better at it, how did they do it? What examples can we find from their experience which would enable us to do the same in our day?

The classic passage dealing with church conflict is Acts 15. It is the account of Paul and Barnabas returning to Jerusalem to report on their missionary activities. To their consternation, they discovered that, while some were encouraged by their report, others wondered if the conversions had been bought too cheaply. It is not an unfamiliar argument in evangelical churches today.

While the Jerusalem situation involved more than one local church, the dynamics of the passage can well be applied to both church-at-large and local church settings in our day.

First, it makes clear that the early church was not always a place of sweetness and light. Even the most casual reading of the New Testament will dispel such wishful thinking.

Nor is it right to believe that the simple way to resolve all conflicts within the church is to pray about them. God forbid that this would be seen to downgrade prayer. It needs to be stressed, however, that before prayer takes place, those who intend to pray need to know what they are praying about. The issues need to be clarified. It is interesting to note how carefully the church at Jerusalem went about doing this.

It is equally obvious that the Holy Spirit was present in this Acts 15 discussion, that engaging in this discussion was not a denial of the presence of the Spirit.

Neither was this a quiet, gentle, passive disagreement. In verse two, the narrative makes clear that Paul and Barnabas were "in sharp dispute" with the group, debating with them. Furthermore, in verse 7 it is noted that "after much discussion," Peter rose to address them. The tone, content and comment of the passage affirms that the discussion was radical and emotional. But it was not personal. They did not debate personalities.

It would have been tempting to challenge Peter about his denial of Jesus or Paul about his persecution of the church or James about his lack of acceptance of his brother. They could have been obsessed with these past failures. They kept to the issue, however, and refused to be sidetracked by destructive behavior. Church conflict which debates at the level demonstrated in this passage ends up with everybody winning.

At first sight, it would appear that the issues of the conflict were different from what might be in dispute in a contemporary local church setting. That, I believe, is a superficial understanding of the passage.

In the first place, an ethnic difference contributed to the

conflict. The "Judaizers" were mostly Jewish in background and Jerusalem-centered, geographically. The people who had been attracted to Christ as a result of the ministry of Paul and Barnabas were mostly either dispersed Jews or Gentiles. The discussion in this passage was about the Gentiles and the grounds for their acceptance by God.

We do not, as a rule, do well in the Christian church at the local level, with ethnic and racial differences. It reflects on us. Rather than celebrating those differences, we barely tolerate them. This is a tragedy for everyone. Those who feel the chill of non-acceptance are hurt. Those who do not fully accept ethnic or racial differences will feel themselves no longer part of the reality of Canada today. It is alienation for everyone and a denial of the God of the New Testament.

In the second place, there was the strong reality of a theological difference. The Judaizers or Pharisees came at it from an Old Testament perspective, arguing that circumcision was a requirement of godly people. Out of that perspective, they argued that the Gentiles must be circumcized in obedience to the law of Moses. Circumcision was seen, from the time of Abraham, as the sign of a true believer. The law of Moses was regarded, by these people, as the statute for all time. Obeying the law of Moses meant more than simply adhering to the Ten Commandments. It meant obeying the ritual law, the food taboos, and the cultural exercises laid down, not only in the first five books of the Bible but in those which had been added by the Pharisees down through the years.

Circumcision and Sabbath observance were the marks of Judaism. It was inconceivable to a devout Jew that a person could be described as "god-fearing" unless that person understood that circumcision and obedience to the law were mandatory. They were not optional extras in their view. This was not a minor dispute for these people. It was central to their whole sense of identity.

There was also a dispute over what we would, today, call *legalism*. The evangelical tradition to which I belong has always seen liberal theology as a major enemy of the faith. I agree with that position. I believe that, too often, liberal theology has sold the store to the lowest bidder. I believe it has frequently cheated people out of a radical diagnosis of their problems—and, consequently, the radical solution which frees them from those problems.

But I must say that legalism was and is every bit as much an enemy as so-called liberalism. "Thou shalt not gamble, smoke or chew/or go with girls who do," expresses something of what has been the theology of legalism marking too much of the evangelical/fundamentalist camp. We become better known for what we are against than what we are for. What a travesty of the gospel.

The Pharisees were so legalistic as to rule that if a tailor went for a walk on the Sabbath—even if he kept to the allowable distance—but accidentally had a needle in his possession, he would have been regarded as a lawbreaker. A whole list of taboos had to be learned, relating to religion, culture and Sabbath observance. The argument at the forefront of this discussion was whether we become acceptable to God because of that kind of obedience. Or was it, as Peter insisted in his speech, that we were saved "because of the grace of the Lord Jesus Christ."

So, while at first sight, the Acts 15 argument seems remote from our day, it is, in point of fact, at the heart of outreach, evangelism and discipleship in today's church. These positive thrusts are often blockaded by ethnic differences, religious disputes and legalism.

The church becomes the enemy. Consumed by prejudice it dimly recognizes, rejecting the very people it claims to want to reach, using its energies to debate irrelevant matters, it sets aside the task to which it is called.

Having identified the ingredients and impact of the dispute, we want, now, to find out the fascinating way in which it was resolved. There would be little point to this exercise if we simply diagnosed, but never prescribed or cured. As we have already noted, there was candid discussion. Peter and James, for example, frankly addressed the issue. Without their intervention, the resulting conclusion would have been different. James, in fact, made the point that "we should not make it difficult for the Gentiles to turn to God."

The candid discussion, in itself, should not cause us anxiety—as long as it does not degenerate into a discussion of the personalities of the people involved. If this key distinction is not observed we end up engaging in self-destruction.

As the discussion proceeded, the group came to understand the crux of the issue. The focal point was put first by the Pharisees, who argued that circumcision was necessary, then by Peter, who enunciated the grace of the Lord Jesus Christ.

The heart of the issue, then, was a theological question focused on the ground by which we become acceptable to God. In the end, the leadership agreed that those grounds were the grace of the Lord Jesus Christ alone. They could not have reached that conclusion unless they had made the effort to clarify the issue.

Before reaching that conclusion, however, there was an appeal to Scripture. James quoted at length from the Old Testament prophet, Amos, chapter 9. In so doing, he points out that in the rebuilding of David's fallen tent, a remnant would seek the Lord. He then proceeds to use that passage to press for the inclusion of "all the Gentiles who bear my name."

James sees, in the Amos passage, that it was always God's intention to use the Jews to bring the Gentiles into the kingdom. This was now actually happening; the evidence of it was before their very eyes. He was appealing to the church to look beyond a narrow Judaism and "not make it difficult for the Gentiles who are turning to God."

James clearly reinforces Peter's concern. They focused on the signs and wonders God had done among the Gentiles. This was, to them, along with the receiving of the Holy Spirit, the basic new element. God was doing something different; they did not bind God to their past experience of him. Their change of mind came about when they went back to Scriptures in the light of their new experience and found that Scripture confirmed this.

It is also both interesting and important to note that there was a willingness to renegotiate the social contract which had existed to this particular time. The contract was that if a Gentile became a god-fearing person, it was mandatory that he or she obey the law of Moses. The end result of this negotiation was an entirely new consensus. It was that Gentile Christians should abstain from food polluted by idols, from sexual immorality, from meats strangled and from blood. The renegotiated contract provided a whole new basis for fellowship and social interaction.

Parenthetically, it is important to note that our Lord, himself, spoke out strongly against sexual immorality. The issue of abstaining from food offered to idols is further discussed in Paul's first letter to the Corinthian church. The question of abstaining from meats strangled and from blood was to enable Jews and Gentiles to eat together without the Jews disqualifying themselves from their cultural heritage.

In resolving the conflict, the leadership of Peter and James was crucial. These men acted together as a bridge, without violating the past, the present or the future. They knitted all three perspectives together, so that people could go away from the meeting, not violated, but with some common unity in the faith.

As the dispute was resolved, there was a deliberate desire to avoid imposing legalistic burdens on the new converts. Peter asked the question, "Why do you try to test God by putting on the necks of the disciples, a yoke that neither we nor our fathers have been able to bear?"

Here, we have a classic means to resolve disputes within the local church. It involves:

• A willingness to discuss things openly, without putting each other down or the introducing of personality differences. There was a high degree of candor.

• A willingness to identify the issue clearly. They clarified the matter under dispute.

• A concern to become biblical Christians, to understand not only what God has said, but what fresh truth we may find in his word which applies to our situation.

• A willingness to negotiate, recognizing that the compromise process does not necessarily produce an inferior Christianity.

It was obviously worth the debate, for out of that discussion, the whole Christian church has prospered, down through the years. The whole Christian cause was liberated to reach the world for Christ. What a wonderful and constructive way to resolve conflict.

Incidentally, once the decision was made, arrangements were made for it to be communicated clearly and decisively. They sent out a deputation of people from the Jerusalem and Antioch churches to Antioch with Paul and Barnabas so that they would have a first hand report of what had taken place. In that deputation, they described Paul and Barnabas as "our dear friends; men who have risked their lives for the name of our Lord Jesus Christ." They endorsed their ministry.

Once the decision was made, they promoted it with enthusiasm. They had come to the conclusion, as a result of this whole process, that the Holy Spirit had spoken. It had been the Spirit in the final analysis, who had reconciled them to not burdening the new believers with anything beyond the minor requirements previously listed.

It was a most helpful and encouraging way to settle a dispute.

It is clear from this passage, therefore, that we do not need to regard disputes within the local church as bad news, or as a sign of spiritual decadence. Not bad news, that is, unless those disputes are bald power struggles involving one person's push for pre-eminence and refusal to give up control.

In this Acts 15 argument, we have a model consisting of a group of believers coming together to face a serious issue. The conflict is serious from the points of view of their past heritage and the progress of the church. They face it as brothers and sisters in Christ, who love and care for each other and are concerned to hear each other out.

Most of all, they, together, are willing for the Lord to do a new thing.

It seems to me that today's church disputes need to be handled in this kind of context. Would to God that they were! If they were, many things which have grown up to divide us would disappear rapidly.

If only we had people of the stature of James and Peter, Paul and Barnabas! They were of strong conviction and personality, taking considerable risks in this kind of debate. They were prepared, however, to put the future of the Lord's work ahead of their own personalities.

Out of their action, they provided us a model for settling

disputes and conflict.

We therefore need to see differences as providing ways to hear each other out, to grow in love for each other and in appreciation for the heart of the Christian faith. They can set the church free for exciting and productive ministry. They can!

God is saying new things to us in the church, today. It would be tragic, as those new things become known, for us not to adopt a process like this. Out of this Acts 15 process, the whole Christian church has prospered. Glory has been brought to the Lord's name.

The challenge for us is to see the same thing happen today.

DEALING WITH
AN UNRESOLVED CONFLICT

Acts 15:36-41

They had such a sharp disagreement that they parted company. Barnabas took Mark and sailed for Cyprus, but Paul chose Silas and left, commended by the brothers to the grace of the Lord. (Acts 15:39, 40)

A young minister unburdened himself during a discussion at a pastor's conference.

"In the church I serve," he said, "there are two prominent members who quarrelled several years ago. They have never reconciled. They will not speak to each other unless it is absolutely unavoidable. It produces tension in the church. It is so bad that nothing will happen in that church until those two make up. Each blames the other and neither will budge."

That young pastor was inexperienced, desperate and concerned. He argued that the behavior of those two church members was a denial of all the Christian church stood for. Not only were they out of fellowship with each other, they were also modelling the opposite of what the church proclaimed.

Whose responsibility was it to change those conditions? The young and inexperienced pastor, the two people at odds with each other or the whole congregation?

My heart went out to the young minister. Here, at the beginning of his calling, he was anxious to see the Lord's work prosper. He was prepared to face the indifference and hostility of the world. He was ill-prepared, however, for the frustration created by the animosity of two stubborn Christians who were poisoning the life of the church he was pastoring. Those two cared more about their own egos than about the Lord and His work.

I have vivid memories of a church member who challenged me on a somewhat similar matter, except that it involved me personally. He came to me one day, saying, "I know you are upset with the Blacks. You feel they are in the wrong and you are in the right. But they are very unhappy. Things are not working out well for them. They won't come back to the church unless you and they are reconciled. Even though you believe it is their fault, not yours, it is your responsibility to take the initiative because of the state they are in."

That set me back on my heels.

My immediate reaction was one of anger and indignation, though, fortunately, I did not express it to the person challenging me. I felt it was unreasonable to put the responsibility on me. My conscience was clear. The people to whom he referred had violated me, not I, them. Their unhappiness was a result of their own actions, not mine. Why should I be the one to initiate reconciliation?

Do you ever react like that?

As I thought and prayed about it, however, I came to believe that the person who challenged me was correct. I wrote to the people who I felt had wronged me, expressing regret at what had caused the breach between us and apologizing for my part in it. I asked if we could meet together and consequently, we did. They received me warmly; we had a long conversation, followed by prayer together. There was personal reconciliation, though it never spilled over to reconciliation with the church. Sadly, they never came back.

What does one do with unresolved conflicts? Obviously, it is desirable to resolve them, for many reasons. Unresolved conflicts represent a burr under the saddle of the church, so to speak, not to mention a contradiction of Scripture.

Such unresolved conflicts come in a variety of forms. The two recounted above are personal and thus, to some extent, reflect a personality problem in one or both of the people involved. The conflict between Paul and Barnabas was largely the same, though family affection and loyalty also played their parts.

Often the conflicts in the church begin in the area of personality. Stubbornness, personal resentment, rivalry for leadership and similar points of friction are the materials out of which the fire is sparked. An otherwise insignificant issue starts it all. The ensuing blaze defies all attempts to quench it.

The New Testament tells us we are to "keep the unity of the Spirit in the bond of peace." Lack of unity in the local church is a serious biblical—and contemporary—issue. It results in energy, which should be directed to more useful ends, being consumed in the dispute. It robs the church of enthusiasm and joy—as well as its reputation.

There is strong evidence that the New Testament views lack of unity as a compelling disaster. Our Lord's own prayer in John 17 was a positive endorsement for unity. The warnings in Titus 3 about causing division are among the most serious in the Bible. Strong disciplinary action was to be taken against those who are contentious. The writer of Titus warns that, if such people continue to be divisive after appropriate warnings, they are to be shunned by the Christian community.

Obviously, unity is desirable, but is it always possible? In itself, is such a question legitimate?

The differences which create disunity are sometimes clearly theological, as they were in the New Testament. The letter to the Galatians contains the classic New Testament references to resolving theological—and other—conflicts.

Sometimes, disputes which begin over theological issues degenerate into personality conflicts. Francis Schaeffer put it so emphatically when he said:

I have observed one thing among true Christians, in their differences, in many countries. What divides and severs true Christian groups, and Christians; what leaves a bitterness which can last 30, 40, 50 or even 60 years in a person's memory, are not the issues of doctrine or belief which cause the difference in the first place. Invariably, it is lack of love, and the bitter things which are said by true Christians in the midst of differences. These stick in the mind like glue. And after time passes and the difference between the Christians or the groups appear less than they did, there are those bitter, bitter things we said in the midst of what we thought was a good and sufficiently objective discussion. These things, these unloving attitudes and words that cause

the stench that the world can smell in the church of Jesus Christ
among those who are really Christians.

I recall, vividly, the feelings of people in another Baptist
church where I pastored. These people attended that church but
would not join it, although they supported it well and were fully
eligible for membership. Indeed, one of those people was a
dear, sweet Christian lady, reasonably prosperous and with a
generous heart for people in both spiritual and economic need.

The reasons associated with the unwillingness of these people to join the church went 40 years into the past. At that time,
in the church where they were then members, there had been a
dreadful quarrel over doctrinal and personality matters. The
quarrel spilled out of a church meeting and into the parking lot
one day, ending in a fist fight. The police had to be called to sort
it out.

That fight left feelings of disillusionment that time never
erased. The "bitter, bitter things" to which Dr. Schaeffer refers
are real and, sometimes, irreversible. His statement, therefore,
is a relevant prelude to our discussion of our Acts 15 text. This
passage tells us about the conflict between Paul and Barnabas; a
sad and tragic difference of personality.

Barnabas was an unusual man. Luke, for his part, was a
friend and associate of Paul, and the writer of the Book of Acts.
He says Barnabas "was a good man, full of the Holy Spirit and
of faith" (Acts 11:24). It was Barnabas who supported Paul and
got him started in his ministry by winning, for him, acceptance
in the church (Acts 11:25).

It is hard to believe that those two men would quarrel.
They had been through so much together. As was noted, it was
Barnabas who gave Saul of Tarsus credibility after his
remarkable conversion on the way to Damascus. When Saul,
later known as Paul, returned to Jerusalem, there was real fear
that his conversion was not real and that its purpose was for him
to infiltrate the Christian community. Barnabas introduced him
to the apostles, took him into his own house and became his col-
league.

Barnabas went with Paul on that first missionary journey.
Together, they were responsible for the church's breaking out

of its restrictive Jewish mold. They lived through the firestorm resulting from their refusal to force the Gentile believers to be circumcised in accordance with Jewish law.

Barnabas and Paul endured open persecution and threats to their lives. Indeed, on one occasion when they were working together, Paul was stoned and left for dead.

Theirs was no casual friendship, but one forged on the anvil of adversity shared, and battles fought and won.

The quarrel on which our passage focuses was centered on Barnabas' nephew, John Mark. We are told that the disagreement between Paul and Barnabas was sharp—and that they parted company.

The cause of the quarrel was an incident which occurred after Paul and Barnabas had left Cyprus and arrived in Perga, a city of Pamphylia. At that point, John Mark left them and returned to Jerusalem for reasons not made obvious in scripture. There appeared to have been an understanding that Mark would stay with the two men until the completion of their mission tour, before returning to Antioch. We do not know if he was homesick, feeling the stress or unwilling to accept the sacrifices of Christian service. But Paul did not want an unreliable person working with them and Barnabas wanted to give his nephew a second chance. In the stress they faced, both men were expressing understandable feelings.

It is less understandable that such mature Christians and good friends allowed the argument to become so personal.

Theirs was a sad and melancholy breach. Did it occur because Paul was too abrasive and Barnabas, too protective?

That question reinforces one posed earlier; it may be desirable to resolve conflict, but is it always possible? One would assume that given Christian commitment and goodwill, it should be possible.

Why, then, did these two men have such difficulty? Was it because it was Barnabas' nature to try to placate? He was known as the "Son of Consolation." Or, was it simply that blood was thicker than water, that John Mark was his nephew and he could overlook his failures for that reason.

It may seem strange to assert that Barnabas' desire to placate was the cause of the dispute. A person who placates

usually tries anything to resolve a conflict. The reason for raising the question is the recognition that a placater is often willing
to go the second and third miles—until something puts him to
the wall. At that point, he or she turns on the person he has been
in the habit of placating. He drops his passive placating role,
switching to angry and abrasive assertions of his own rights. In
Barnabas' case, family kinship could have been the trigger to set
off his change in behavior. There has to be some explanation.

As for the Apostle Paul, our reading of him could cause us
to ask whether he was much too tough in conflict situations,
better at escalating conflict than resolving it. This may be an unfair characterization of Paul, but it is a common one.

Whatever the reason for the Paul-Barnabas conflict, the
early church came to the conclusion that it was better for Paul
and Barnabas to separate and go their own ways. The church
did not resolve this particular conflict. The passage describing it
is a simple and obvious reminder that it is not always possible to
resolve conflict, no matter how hard we try or how deeply committed we are to its resolution. That axiom is true in marriage,
in the wider family, and—sometimes—in the local church.

We have noted from the New Testament that there are
times when a person is so contentious by nature that the only
thing to do is discipline him and let him go. Quite specifically,
Titus says, "Avoid foolish controversies . . . arguments and
quarrels about the law, because they are unprofitable and
useless. Warn a divisive person once. Warn him a second time.
After that, have nothing to do with him. You may be sure that
such a man is warped and sinful; he is self-condemned."

Titus, of course, is referring to an extreme situation, when
a person's contentiousness is so ingrained as to cause havoc in
the local church. He says the time comes when one must give up
on that kind of person, to give him to the Lord and let him be,
to put him out of the fellowship and get on with one's life.

This is, however, hardly the proper understanding of the
conflict between Paul and Barnabas. It involved two well-
respected servants of God—not the kinds of warped and sinful
people to whom Titus referred. The conflict was unresolved, in
their case. Could it be because of their pride and stubbornness?
When we find ourselves prevented by our pride and stubborn-

ness from being reconciled with our brother, the pride must go. What are we to do if the brother or sister will not respond? Surely, we must get on with the rest of our lives.

It is not always possible to reconcile because wilfulness, incompatibility, arrogance—whatever—prevents reconciliation from taking place. The early church, in the case of Paul and Barnabas, wisely decided to get on with life, and not to prolong a futile reconciliation attempt. Both men were commended by the brothers to the grace of the Lord and were sent off to do their work. Paul and Silas went to Syria; Barnabas and Mark returned to Cyprus.

The story of the Paul-Barnabas conflict turns Acts 15 into a strange mixture. As we have noted, it begins with an intense debate. One translation uses the expression, "a fierce argument." The two men work through their dispute and eventually reach an agreement which has lasted close to 2,000 years. Paul and Barnabas were theological allies. Their friendship was a remarkable achievement. Yet this chapter ends with these very men unable to reconcile over what seems an unimportant matter—whether to take John Mark on their missionary journey.

The church presumably attempted to reconcile the two men, found it impossible and sent them both off with different partners to serve the Lord.

Is there a message in this incident for us?

Could it be that if you find yourself in such a situation, you are not expected to spend the rest of your energies trying to reconcile the irreconcilable? When it is a personality matter, rather than a question of principle, it is not worth that energy. It would appear that you have New Testament grounds for this kind of reaction.

We do not know the end of this story. Hopefully, one day, Paul and Barnabas wrote each other, assuring the other of their oneness, love and support. We know, at least, that later on, Paul and John Mark were reconciled; the assumption may be that so were Paul and Barnabas. Time is a great healer. Paul writes in 2 Timothy 4:11, "Get Mark and bring him with you, because he is helpful to me in my ministry."

It is clear also, that following this particular phase of their lives, John Mark wrote the gospel which bears his last name. We may rest assured that neither Paul, Silas, Barnabas or John Mark allowed this quarrel to dominate their lives.

They got on with the rest of their lives.

There are times when we need to do the same.

At such a time, when we have done all within our power to resolve the conflict, we must not let an unreconciled person dominate our personal agenda—or even our local church agenda.

Therefore, to the question of the desirability of reconciliation, the answer is a resounding "yes!" But, to the question of its possibility, it may be "alas, no." Romans 12:18 says "as much as lieth within you, live peaceably with all men." So we do what is within our power. Having done so, we give the matter over to the Lord. Then we proceed to enjoy our lives and serve Him.

Unresolved conflicts are never good news. But to allow a conflict you have honestly sought before God to resolve to dominate your life, is even worse.

Don't let it happen to you.

This passage indicates that several steps are involved in dealing with personality conflicts.

In the first instance, reconciliation is a primary goal. It is not acceptable for Christians to refuse to make up. This is the heart of the Christian message. We must model what we proclaim.

When it is impossible to reach reconciliation because the issue between the parties is so evenly balanced, the church has a role to play. Church leaders need to do all in their power to bring the parties together. Pleading, persuading and confronting are all legitimate strategies.

If all that fails, the implication of this passage is that, rather than wasting energy, it is more important to let the people involved alone. It is almost like saying, "A plague on both your houses; we are going to get on with the Lord's work."

Just two matters should be added.

First, if an individual is constantly creating personality conflict in the family or the church, that person needs to be confronted and disciplined.

Next and, perhaps, more important, is how a person wanting to be reconciled handles himself if the other person refuses conciliatory overtures. The answer to that question depends on the seriousness of the cause of the original dispute, and who was responsible. Even if the cause was serious and you are at fault, the fact that you are seriously attempting reconciliation is to your credit.

It may be understandable, if the offence was serious, that the other person is reluctant to be reconciled. This would be particularly so, if you were into a pattern of behaviour that had been destructive to them. In such a case, you would need to demonstrate some long term behavior changes. Assuming there had not been destructive behavior, the fact that you have genuinely sought to be reconciled is important. It may not be enough to obtain the reconciliation, but it is enough to show good faith on your part.

Having made an honest and sincere attempt, you must not allow the failure of the other person to respond to dominate your life. At that point, you need to get on with the rest of your life. Leave the door to reconciliation open but do not use massive amounts of spiritual energy trying to force the situation.

Barnabas and Mark went off to Cyprus; Paul and Silas to Syria. As far as we know, both sets of people had productive lives and ministries.

Why not do the same?

AN ANGRY CONFRONTATION: IS IT EVER JUSTIFIED?

Galatians 2:11-13

When Peter came to Antioch, I opposed him to his face, because he was in the wrong. Before certain men came from James, he used to eat with the Gentiles. But when they arrived, he began to draw back and separate himself from the Gentiles because he was afraid of those who belonged to the circumcision group. The other Jews joined him in his hypocrisy, so that by their hypocrisy even Barnabas was led astray.

Have you ever had a letter from someone who was so angry with you that it almost scorched the page? Perhaps you have even written such an epistle.

I have received one or two such letters, fewer than I deserved, no doubt. In reality, though, the angry letters I have received have accused me of crimes which, fortunately, I could prove I had not committed. The writers did not know the offences that I was really guilty of, for which I have been devoutly thankful!

The New Testament contains an angry letter. One can imagine the papyrus of the day scorching as the Apostle Paul wrote his searing words. It is the Letter to the Galatians. At the beginning, the writer uses a term that the King James translates as "anathema"—an ultimately strong word of censure. The New International Version simply states, "If we or an angel from heaven should preach a gospel other than the one we preach to you, let him be condemned." In case the point was missed, Paul repeats himself, "As we have already said, so I say again: If anybody has preached to you a gospel other than what you have already accepted, let him be eternally condemned."

Whether you prefer an anathema to being eternally con-

demned is a matter of personal choice. Neither description is to
be desired.

There is no polite introduction to this letter, no polished attempt to soften up the Galatians so they can hear what Paul has
to say. There are no nice illustrations to arouse their sym-
pathies. There are direct, clear, angry statements.

The letter is quite diffferent in style from most of our accepted methods of handling things. Mostly, in Canada, an attempt would be made to provide some positive comments. We
would try to warm up to the situation. The abrupt, abrasive
"head-on" approach would not be favored. Clearly, Paul was
too upset about the matter to be urbane and polite. The importance of the issue caused him to take Peter on directly, without
any ambiguities or attempts at diplomacy.

Paul talks about people "perverting the gospel of Christ"
(Galatians 1:7). Continuing, he claims, "The gospel I preach is
not something that man made up . . . I received it by revelation
from Jesus Christ." He argues that "false brothers have in-
filtrated our ranks to spy out the freedom we have in Christ"
(2:4). Again, note the language: "Peter . . . in his hypocrisy"
(2:13).

Galatians is a remarkable book. The first part of it is filled
with heavy accusations and strong language, as strong as the
Christian community could be expected to permit.

Yet the book is also the manifesto of Christian freedom.
One of the New Testament's most famous statements, in fact, is
contained in Galatians, "There is neither Jew nor Greek,
slave nor freed, male nor female, for you are all one in Christ
Jesus" (3:28). That statement is used to argue not simply the
freedom of slaves but the emancipation of women—as well as
the annihilation of ethnic and racial barriers. The book also
notes that "it is for freedom that Christ has set us free" (5:1).

The book illustrates our 20th century difficulty with Paul.
At first sight, he appears abrasive, narrow, legalistic and
ungenerous. But once we get behind his way of expressing
himself, we find him generous, progressive and never narrow or
legalistic. His plea for Christian freedom in this strongly-
worded book is the cause of his blunt words.

So Galatians is not simply a polemic, an angry letter written so Paul could sound off after being caught in a bad mood. It is a book which he uses to argue issues which, to him, are of crucial importance.

How could Paul have used such violent language, anyway, in his angry confrontation with Peter, as recounted in our text? While we rejoice to know what he says about freedom, we wonder if he is denying, by the language and statements used in the early chapters, the very points he is asserting.

A confrontation as extreme as this raises some questions which require answering. The first question is, "Is the statement true?" If it is not true, there is no issue. If it is, then concern is important.

In our culture, the question regarding truth is not often the first one asked. Our questions are: "Is it convenient?", "Is it self-satisfying?", "Is it awkward?", "Will it create problems?", or "What will be the damage?" While all these questions are important, they were never, for Paul, the major concerns. In our society, we have grown to be afraid of the question, "Is it true?"

I recall being part of a television panel moderated by Charles Templeton. When we were rehearsing, I was arguing for the Christian position on an issue. Before he could stop himself, Templeton responded by saying, "I didn't want to ask Pilate's question but I will. What is truth?"

It is a sad commentary on our times that such a question is rarely asked.

It is so easy to be betrayed by one's own bias. Some of us, out of our ethnic origin, family background, our genes, or some such reason, love the battle. We are easily manipulated into conflict. The story of the church is one replete with controversies which had as much or more to do with personality as with important theological issues. Some of us are far too ready to believe the worst of other people, because of our own needs, feelings of inadequacy or unresolved guilt. We fall into personality conflict so quickly that we hardly know we have moved from a matter of wider significance to one which is basically personal.

Personality does not appear to be a major factor in the confrontation set within the book of Galatians. There are, however, elements of it. In Galatians 2:9, for example, Paul speaks of "James, Peter and John; those reputed to be pillars." His phraseology is not that of a person expressing himself concerning the three men with warmth and affection, but rather with a touch of skepticism about their "reputed" status. Perhaps he is feeling a bit upset with how easily they seem to have been accepted. They appear to have avoided the battle he felt he was trapped into. His acceptance was never easy.

But the issues here go well beyond personality. The controversy is a reflection of the agreement made in Acts 15, between Paul and Barnabas on one hand, and the church at Jerusalem, on the other. That agreement saw James and Peter actively supporting Paul in the issue he is now concerned about. The argument, as we outlined in a previous chapter, was created by the expansion of the church and the conversion of many Gentiles. With that expansion came the contention of the Judaizers that the new believers should observe the details of the Jewish food regulations, and other similar cultural redundancies. These regulations, it should be remembered, were not based simply on the Old Testament but on additional rules added by the Jewish community through the centuries.

Behind that, however, was an even bigger matter: that relating to what one must do to win God's acceptance. If faith in Jesus Christ and his death on the cross was not sufficient, what then needs to be added? The Judaizers argued that one must observe the Jewish law. But Paul and, eventually, the Christian church in Jerusalem maintained that to add these elements would be to deny the sufficiency of the death of Christ.

Peter's hypocrisy, as articulated by Paul in Galatians 2:11, was that he was reneging on the agreement reached in Acts 15. The agreement made it possible for Jewish Christians to eat with Gentile Christians. Not only had he reneged, he had also persuaded Barnabas, a Cypriot, to do the same. Because he did not want to offend the Jews, he had lost sight of the heart of the gospel.

Paul had his facts straight. By forcing the Gentile Christians to accept Jewish customs, Peter had added a burden which the Jewish Christians themselves could not bear. They were, in fact, arguing that justification came not by faith in Christ but by observing the law. As Paul so clearly pointed out, that was a denial of the heart of the gospel.

From there, Paul proceeds to enunciate that conviction. "The life that I live in the body," he says, "I live by faith in the Son of God who loved me and gave himself for me. I do not set aside the grace of God. For if righteousness could be gained through the law, Christ died for nothing" (2:20, 21).

Without doubt, we must answer in the affirmative, the question about the validity and importance of the issue Paul is dealing with here. If we are agreed that Paul was right about the issue, we need to ask some further questions.

We should ask, for example, if being right is enough. It is possible to have one's facts straight, yet still be inappropriate, unfair and unjustified in taking an issue to the extreme. You can be "off the wall," as one contemporary expression puts it. Finding out about the truth is only the beginning.

Two other related questions Christians need to ask—and often—are: "Is it just or fair to make such a big issue of this matter?" and "Can the conflict be worth the cost involved?"

Failure to ask those questions has cost us dearly in terms of Christian unity, both in the local church and in the church-at-large. So many conflicts are not worth the battle fought to win them. When the people who fought them won, they lost; when they lost, they lost, too.

For example, Baptists and Canadians at large have paid dearly for the 1920s controversies over the kind of theological education students were receiving at McMaster Divinity School, the Baptist seminary on the McMaster University campus in Hamilton, Ontario. The issues permanently split the Baptist communion in Canada. To this day, those who have inherited the polarization in Baptist life continue to blame each other's side for the split. The argument over the allegations that liberal theology was being taught at McMaster created a continuing bitter contention. One of the consequences of that controversy has been a poisoning of Baptist life in Canada which remains as bitter as ever.

But beyond the effect on Baptists themselves has been the negative influence on Canada as a nation. That has occurred because Baptists have spent much of their energy fighting each other, instead of raising a voice in national affairs. Canada has lacked a strong mainline denominational voice with a committed evangelical position: a voice which Baptists could have provided.

This kind of conflict can be ugly and destructive. Its long term effects go far beyond what the original protagonists could have foreseen. The questions, "Does it really matter?" and "Will the price to be paid make it worth it?" are significant.

We need to make a kind of spiritual cost-benefit analysis of conflicts, both in the larger church and in individual situations. I was talking recently with a couple, good friends of ours, who have had a running battle for some time, on seemingly unimportant issues. They have argued as to whether the bedroom window should be opened or closed, whether the curtains should be drawn or pulled. They argue about whether it is selfish for one to read in bed and possibly disturb the other. After 30 years of marriage, they have failed to resolve these issues and they remain contentious matters between them. But they are hardly the kinds of issues worth 30 years of unresolved conflict.

Too many arguments are over questions which are trivial in the long term. In many evangelical churches, for example, there are arguments about what part, if any, women may play in worship. Apparently, they may sing, but not talk. They may perform, but not pray audibly. They may visit on behalf of the church, but they may not be deacons or elders. I am not arguing, in this instance, about the rights and wrongs of the issue, but making the point that the particular distinctions drawn are beyond my understanding. (The truth is that, at times, music conveys the gospel more effectively than speech.)

Paul's argument, advanced in Galatians 2, was, nevertheless, no unimportant trivial concern. It was at the very heart of the Christian faith itself, because it brought to the surface the great fact of redemption; Christ's work on the cross was sufficient for my salvation and God's acceptance of me. From the Christian perspective, there can be no question of greater significance than that. Anything which was added to what Christ did for us, in effect, diminished his actions on our behalf.

In that sense, then, Peter's action—adding baggage to the

Christian's quest for acceptance with God, after having already agreed not to—was hypocrisy. Further, he went beyond ordinary denial to a *de facto* denial of the faith itself, by acting in a way which deceived people about what he really believed.

It may very well be true that Peter did not intend such a denial, but, in this instance, his lack of bad intentions do not help. He was lending his enormous prestige to a group of people for whom being Jewish was more important than being Christian. He did not, himself, believe that, but his actions reinforced it. Peter found it difficult to take a stand that was unpopular or personally threatening.

Peter's weakness was first shown when, under questioning at the time of Jesus' arrest, he denied his Lord. That weakness now reasserts itself.

In one respect, it is encouraging that a person as wonderful as Peter could battle with this weakness all his life, losing sometimes but able to make a comeback. But it is ominous, too, and discouraging, to see the weakness recur. On that basis, Paul's anger was justified.

Having agreed that Paul had a right to be angry, we come to the third set of questions to be considered: "Was the issue important enough to warrant what was said?" "Did Paul go about expressing his anger in the right way?"

Do any of us, in fact, express our anger appropriately?

To the extent that we have pointed out where the importance of the issue lay, we have already partially answered those questions. If we can agree that the Acts 15 discussion predates the Galatians dispute, then we can understand that Paul was not responding for the first time to the issue. Acts 15 consisted of a whole process: the report brought to the Jerusalem church, the sharp and strong debate, the intervention by both Peter and James on the side which Paul was advocating, the compromise reached on non-essential issues and, finally the signing of an agreement hammered out by all parties.

Furthermore, in Acts 15, the parties had worked out a method to implement the recommendation, the end product of long debate.

When Paul angrily confronted the issue in his letter to the Galatians, he had already exhausted all the alternatives. He needed to act quickly and directly, as he saw it. The danger was not simply that some individuals were being led astray, but that the whole strategy of the church would perish. He believed that if the battle was lost, all the benefits of the Christian faith would be lost along with them.

This, then, was no simple, straightforward personal animosity toward Peter. Paul had been through so much from the group whom Peter was placating. Some of their friends and allies had pursued him with the intention of killing him. But significant as this may have been for him, personally, it was not the heart of the concern.

And he was right to have that concern. Indeed, the church itself would have perished. The benefits of the gospel, direct and indirect, would have disappeared for all time.

This can be illustrated in today's world by looking at the effect of the gospel in what we commonly call "the third world." Despite their obvious difficulties, many third world or less developed nations would be worse off than they are, if the church had perished. It is not popular to draw attention to the benefits of Christian mission and third world development today. Agreed, there is room for criticism of the church's westernization in underdeveloped countries. We need to accept, however, that those things which make life tolerable in many third world nations begin with the effect of the Christian gospel.

The reality cannot be ignored, for example, that most of the leaders of the emerging African nations received at least part of their education as a direct result of the missionary movement. Furthermore, in many of those countries, the beginning of written language comes out of this Christian commitment. The list continues: human rights, political freedom, the codes of law—aside entirely from what is primarily important to the Christian faith, a knowledge of God in Christ. All of these benefits would have been lost, had Paul not prevailed in this particular argument.

It was for that very reason that Paul was direct, unequivocal, unmistakable in his language and totally unprepared for compromise. He went for it and he was right.

Before we find ourselves imitating Paul, however, we need to imitate his process, to see that all previous avenues have been explored before confronting such an issue. Failure to do so creates a destructive force which is both immense and almost irreversible. We are dealing, here, with an issue within the Christian community which may be rare but is not absent. Even in our day, we face the possibility of church groups becoming apostate by their denial of the fundamentals of the faith and their unwillingness to recognize what constitutes the heart of the gospel. The issue Paul raises in the Galatian letter is not dead.

In such an internal church conflict, how are we to handle ourselves?

We need to see that, at times, an issue is so serious that not to confront it is to be morally and spiritually irresponsible. It is not appropriate to disguise such a concern with polite or bland words.

How can we know, though, when an issue has reached such a point?

We need to remind ourselves of the preliminary questions to be asked.

The first is, "How do I normally react to that person or group?" If the truth of the matter is that I do not really like them, then I should stop, because I am not in a position to get involved in that controversy. My own attitude will unfairly bias the way in which it is conducted, preempting any possibility of understanding and reconciliation. If I find that I feel myself to be an outsider, with the naturally accompanying sense of alienation, then, again, I need to deal with that question, before getting into a difficult, serious and complicated controversy.

The second question is: "How do I normally handle conflict?" Am I the kind of person who likes to go for the jugular, who loves controversy? Or am I the kind of passive aggressive person who likes to lie in the bushes for a while, then suddenly attack violently? I need to know how I will handle a conflict before I become involved in a serious controversy. Perhaps someone else is more equipped than I am to handle the confrontation; my role is to pray that God will send that person.

A fascinating paragraph in Martyn Lloyd-Jones' autobiography recounts a visit Lloyd-Jones received from T.T. Shields. Shields is the late longtime minister of Toronto's Jarvis Street Baptist Church. He was the chief protagonist for the fundamentalist side of the McMaster Divinity School controversy. Lloyd-Jones, who was an outstanding British expositor, became concerned over Shields' polemical approach. He believed that Shields, whom he viewed as a magnificent expositor of Scripture, was prejudicing his ministry with his penchant for controversy.

Shields listened to what Lloyd-Jones had to say but, in the end, did not heed his advice.

If he had chosen, instead, to take that advice, what a difference it would have made to church history in Canada. That gifted man would have been more self-aware. He would have been able to realize that his love for controversy apparently outweighed his passionate concern for particular issues.

The third question is: "How important is the issue?" Where is it on a scale of one to ten? A "one" could be rated as an issue where it matters not whether it is ever settled—like my friends' open bedroom window. A "ten" may well concern the eternal destiny of human beings. I need to make that kind of evaluation. If it is not a "ten" then I need to be careful that the controversy does not become so heated that I jeopardize people's eternal destinies by my actions, when the issue itself would not have done so.

If the answer is a "ten," however, then it is clear to me that I must start to exhaust all the other remedies: persuasion, understanding, listening and discussion without anger or bitterness. I must not act in haste—yet neither can I evade the issue. It is clear, too, that it has reached the point where compromise is more destructive than the issue itself.

That penchant for compromise on vital issues is, in some ways, a Canadian difficulty. The up-side of Canadian life is our unwillingness to get involved in bitter controversies which have dogged other communities. When faced with an issue which has been imported from overseas, we tend to say, "Let them fight their own battles back home. We do not want them to do it here." The down-side is that our failure to get to the heart of the issue costs us dearly in the end.

Obviously, there are times when with fear, trembling, self-examination, prayer and consultation with other mature believers, an issue becomes important enough to broach in the way Paul did in Galatians 2.

I fear greatly that in Canadian church life, we are drifting into situations which require some careful confrontation. Some of the social concerns of the United Church of Canada, for example, are vital to be heard. But the willingness to ordain ministers regardless of their sexual orientation has the makings of a spiritual tragedy—for the United Church itself and for the Christian cause in Canada. This question is precipitating a serious biblical and theological crisis in our situation.

Hopefully, as this issue moves to the crisis level, people in the Christian community who are concerned about it will go through the process I described earlier, so that if we get to the point of a head-on conflict, it will be because we were driven by events, not because of a love of controversy.

There is a real danger, in Canada, that we could end up failing to deal with issues which reach the heart of the Christian gospel, compromising, in the end, so willingly and in such a way that no one will hear the gospel itself.

An angry confrontation is, at times, both necessary and justified. But we had better end it with reluctance and clear self-understanding. There will need to be careful prayer that we will conduct ourselves with a desire to glorify God and exercise genuine Christian love.

You may be upset with the anger that confrontation engenders. Why can't it be civilized, controlled, polite and gentle? Surely not to be angry when somebody is causing confusion concerning the most vital and important issue in life is to be responding inadequately. Failure to be angry can be a reflection of indifference. To be indifferent when someone is deceiving others about the terms on which God accepts us is hardly virtuous.

If you never get angry over vital and important issues, what do you think that says about you?

There are moments, however rare, when the battle needs to be joined, and, under God, won.

CONFRONTING CONFLICT IN CANADIAN SOCIETY

Matthew 22:21

Give to Caesar what is Caesar's and to God, what is God's.

Almost daily, it seems, new conflicts surface in Canadian society. The old days, in which there was a consensus or a social contract, are gone, apparently forever. Not only is there conflict between evangelical Christianity (of which I am a part) and the rest of Canadian society, but conflicts within that whole society.

In Alberta, recently, for example, there arose a dispute between the United Appeal and the labour unions, as a result of which the Unions withdrew their support from the UA. They based their withdrawal on grounds that some of the organizations funded through the United Appeal obtained government contracts thus depriving government union workers of jobs. While there was some basis in fact for the unions' argument, it also remains that many innocent people suffered from the shortfall of funds caused by their withdrawal.

That conflict is symptomatic of the breakdown we find in society—and the conflicts leading to and arising from those breakdowns.

I wish, at this point, however, to focus on the conflict between evangelical Christians and society at large. In particular, I would like us to consider how evangelical Christians should live and act within a world influenced by these conflict-induced changes. The present issues which put evangelicals into conflict with the rest of society are exemplified by disagreements over whether sexual orientation is a basic civil right or whether the government should support REAL Women. It is impossible to predict what the conflicts may be tomorrow.

We have gone through a 20-year period in which all the

positions which were once strongly held by the Christian community—and by most Canadians—are being demolished. Evangelical Christians, in particular, once considered Canada to be a nominally Christian country. Many now believe the opposite to be the case.

Many perspectives are changing in our society. For example, the distribution and consumption of alcohol has been a traditional bone of contention between evangelical Christians and the rest of Canadian society. Rightly or wrongly, that is no longer so. The concern over the abuse of alcohol is now expressed through organizations like Mothers Against Drunk Drivers.

That issue has been replaced with a whole set of concerns, including prostitution, pornography, abortion and Sunday shopping. Those concerns represent only the tip of the iceberg. Below the surface are Christian concerns about the apparent bias of key national decision-makers against traditional family values. Such concerns turn to real fear when church leaders wonder if they will be subject to criminal prosecution if, for example, they decline to hire people for church staffs whose sexual orientation they consider to be contrary to biblical teaching.

There is no doubt that a serious rift has opened up in Canadian society and is unlikely to go away. The social contract has been breached and consensus has come to an end. The depth and width of the breach is illustrated by the political powerlessness that Christians of all kinds are experiencing. It was, for example, a Liberal minister of justice, John Turner, who opened the door, some 15 years ago, to the changes in the Criminal Code allowing for abortion. Further, the proposal to create special rights for homosexuals appears to have the consent of a Conservative prime minister, Brian Mulroney. Both men are serious, practising Roman Catholics.

Unless there is a dramatic spiritual revival, it is clear that the pace of the development of a secular society in Canada will continue to accelerate. Schools, for example, are increasingly forbidden to include specifically Christian elements in their programs, even—and especially—at Christmas. The university, the school, the hospital, the various social agencies and now government itself, regardless of political affiliation, appear set on dismantling the Christian apparatus and imposing a secular mindset on the community. Christian convictions are increasingly seen as irrelevant, obsolete—and more ominously, perhaps—politically unimportant.

Obviously, our politicans do not see themselves as moral pacesetters! It would be hoped, however, that people who profess a faith would allow that faith and the teachings of their church to help shape the decisions they make. If I read the Mulroney and Turner examples correctly, they appear to believe there is no political or moral penalty for the positions they take on the issues I pinpointed. Indeed, they must be aware that the political penalty for not making these concessions is one to be feared.

The question arises, therefore, as to how we should respond to this new and destructive situation.

Should Christians see secularization simply in terms of its threat to our influence and power? Surely not. We need to see beyond that point, to where such influences are threatening to the values which make community possible.

It is understandable that politically active people are upset when they lose political clout. To make that a major concern, however, is to function as if political power is more important than moral conviction. That, surely, is an attitude to be feared.

We need to see those trends as a denial and rejection of the God of the Bible. That, for us, is a calamity.

It is not easy to know how to react. There is no doubt that Canadian society is more pluralistic than it has ever been before. There are provinces, for example, where followers of the Sikh religion outnumber such traditionally-settled groups as Baptists or Presbyterians. We are into an entirely and radically different era.

How do Christians live and act in such a society? How can we insist on our rights in a multicultural, pluralistic society, where the community-at-large sees all religions as equal—and the Christian religion as less equal than others?

The secularizing trend, in fact, has caused some Christians to take to the streets. They exercise their rights as citizens to protest vigorously. They picket. They make very clear in as public a form as possible, their objection to what is happening.

They see in Jeremiah, who walked the streets of Jerusalem with a wooden yoke on his shoulders, a model of social protest.

Others are involved in what they see to be a more thoughtful and careful approach to government. The Evangelical Fellowship of Canada, under the leadership of the Rev. Brian Stiller, is a typical example of this approach. But there is not a substantial amount of success to record at this point in time. Even those ministers of government sympathetic to the Christian faith appear to have no decisive influence, when push comes to shove, on issues of concern to the evangelical Christian community.

Others, still, withdraw into the Christian ghetto, leaving the world to look after itself. That hardly seems a productive position for a Christian to take. Such people feel, quite sincerely, that we should walk the second mile rather than resist. Their sincerity is to be admired, their prayer life to be coveted. But is withdrawal a proper response?

Yet others appear to sell out the Christian gospel so that they can accommodate themselves to society, to gain popularity or privilege. They are, perhaps, least successful of all, in asserting a Christian presence in secular society. They are left not only with the realization that they have deserted their fellow Christians but with the contempt of others who know they sold out. They are in double jeopardy, to say nothing of their ultimate accounting to the Lord.

We need to ask how New Testament Christians managed to live and leave their mark in an alien society, even more adamantly opposed to Christian conviction than we are today.

Despite the decline in Christian influence and values in Canada, we still face a less hostile society than did those believers whose pilgrimages are recorded in the pages of the New Testament.

To start with, we can optimistically record that New Testament Christians survived, propagated the faith, confronted society—and were neither depressed nor dismayed by the process. The New Testament has much to say about the duties of the citizen; the word from our Lord in today's text is one prominent example.

It is true that the world of the New Testament was radically different from our own. Citizenship was confined to the elite. Women had no power, politically or otherwise. Slavery was normal.

Nevertheless, the Roman peace prevailed, and that in itself produced enormous gratitude, considering the general conditions in the world of Jesus' time. The one exception to the Roman influence was the strong Jewish nationalism and its commitment to the God of the Old Testament.

Apart from that Jewish nationalism, people were reasonably content with Roman rule. Make no mistake, though. They were not living in a democracy, as we are. The citizen had little recourse, as do we, though he might try to petition the emperor, with the remote chance of getting his attention. Even if that attention was gained, it was not likely to be productive for the petitioner. Paul could bear living testimony to that reality—even if the use of the word *living* is inappropriate.

So we return to our question: What does it mean to render to Caesar what is Caesar's and to God, what is God's? Indeed, what is Caesar's and what is God's?

This incident, repeated in all three of the synoptic gospels, has been perceived differently by various commentators. In his book, *An Exegetical Commentary on the Gospel, According to St. Matthew*, Alfred Plummer observed that the question about tribute was reasonable, one on which a rabbi of great repute might be asked his opinion.

Nevertheless, Plummer points out that the gospel writers saw this question not as one asked to elicit information, but to embarrass and trouble Jesus. He argues that the coin that was produced by Jesus' questioners represented "Roman organization, security of person and property, facilities of transit and other munificent elements of stable government." Therefore, to render to Caesar was not merely a lawful obligation but a moral one, in such a society. He sees this as an example of our Lord's pragmatism and concern for civil stability.

Others have argued that Jesus, for his own best reasons, was simply evading the question. He did not want to be diverted from his purpose by addressing the matter.

Yet others believe Jesus was giving blanket endorsement to the state. It is the citizen's responsibility, they would argue, to obey the state, no matter what its demands may be. Some Christians in the Soviet Union accept that stance, so do some of their American counterparts. They believe the state is right, patriotism is a virtue and love for and loyalty to one's country is endorsed by Christ.

It would seem, however, that our Lord's comment is part of a New Testament pattern. In that pattern, it is recognized that there are two kingdoms, one which is of God, the other, of the civil world. Further, the New Testament recognizes that the two kingdoms have differing functions, each requiring its own form of respect. It accepts that we should render to Caesar what, in fact, is Caesar's right.

In Romans 13, for example, the principle is taken much further. Words and statements in that chapter appear to endorse the position of those who would have us respect the state regardless. It begins by saying everyone must submit himself to the governing authorities for there is no authority except that which God has established. And if that is not made clear enough, Paul continues by noting, "He who rebels against the authority is rebelling against what God has instituted and those who do so, bring open judgment upon themselves."

Later in the passage, regarding the state, he says, "He is God's servant to do you good. But if you do wrong, be afraid, for he does not bear the sword for nothing. He is God's servant, an agent of wrath to bring punishment on the wrongdoer." On this basis Paul concludes that we pay taxes to the authorities because they are God's servants and we give to each what we owe him—taxes, revenue, respect and honor.

Does this mean that every ruler is God's servant? It would be hard to accept that premise. In the Roman society to which Paul wrote, Nero was hardly regarded as a conscious servant of the Lord. In our day it would be very difficult to persuade Ugandan Christians to believe that their autocratic former president, Idi Amin, was God's servant, an agent of wrath to bring punishment on the wrongdoer. Indeed, the punishment inflicted by Idi Amin was on the Christian community.

Is Paul simply arguing that government is ordained by God? That when government fulfills its task as ordained by God, that we should respect it, see it as an agent of God? Surely he does not touch, in this passage, on what to do when government is clearly an agent of the devil, as we have seen so often in today's world. Nevertheless, the least that we can understand these passages as saying, is that there is a duty on the part of the citizen to obey the governing powers and to render to Caesar what is his. It may not always be easy to know what in fact does belong to Caesar; but what does belong to him must, to him, be rendered.

The passages do not help us as much as we would like, to understand how to react in a democratic society to a government which is undercutting the Christian view of life—and expects Christian support for the process.

What is the effect of the choices made by Christians today?

One approach is the attempt to force society to conform to the Christian ethic. Christian leaders who advance this approach argue that whether the majority is for or against a particular issue, its very rightness commends it. Further, they insist that the Christian ethic should be enforced whether the community approves it or not. The difficulty is that such an approach has never worked and when it has been tried, the result has been enormously destructive.

No less a person than John Stott in his book *Issues Facing Christians Today*, reminds us, for example, of the way in which the Spanish Inquisition functioned. Christian society, at that time and in that setting, had an apparent majority. Impenitent heretics "were punished by excommunication, imprisonment and confiscation of goods, then were handed over to the state to be burned alive. All Christian traditions are deeply ashamed that such methods should ever have been used in the name of Jesus Christ."

All Christians, says Stott, affirm that totalitarianism and torture are both wholly incompatible with the mind and spirit of Jesus.

He continues by recounting the effects of prohibition in the United States. He regards those attempts to impose belief and behavior as unproductive and, in fact, destructive. In a world like ours, he argues, we cannot force Christian convictions in that fashion. And I would agree.

That agreement, however, is reluctant. The argument that

Christian behavior is the best behavior and that society itself benefits from its implementation, is accurate. The difficulty is that a commitment to democracy carries with it the obligation not to coerce and compel. In addition, the experience of following such Christian action is scarcely encouraging.

The second alternative is perhaps the opposite: to recognize that we live in a pluralistic society, should be tolerant of the views of others and should not strive to see Christian views prevail. On issues like pornography, prostitution and sexual orientation, to use some examples, we should not be insistent. We have to live and let live.

I remember being at a consultation arranged by the Canadian Broadcasting Corporation, where the senior staff of the CBC was present with a small group of religious leaders. In that discussion, a CBC executive, whose name is a household word, responded to one of my comments by stating, "You must recognize that you now live in a pluralistic society and you cannot expect your views to dominate." I responded by noting that I respected the reality of living in a pluralistic society—but that I wanted to know when our share of the pluralism would be demonstrated by the CBC. He gave mental assent to my reaction but showed little inclination, at that time, to follow through on my concern.

There is no disputing the fact that we live in a pluralistic society in Canada. There are likely as many followers of the "new age" movement in Canada as there are evangelical Christians—or more. The populations of those who follow Hinduism, Buddhism or Islam have reached significant numbers. There is little doubt that the secular humanist dominates the political process.

We must accept reality. It will not hurt us to be less arrogant in expressing our views. We certainly must live and let live. But silence cannot be condoned where evil is obviously being promoted. There is a need for prophetic voice in our kind of society and world. We have surely learned that, at least, from the history of the first half of the twentieth century.

Hitler's ability to take over Germany and enforce his position, grew, in part, out of the failure of the church of that day to speak out prophetically. There were some voices raised—Karl

Barth, Paul Tillich, Dietrich Bonhoeffer among them—but, by and large, the church was silent. Bonhoeffer, in his anger, charged, "The evangelical church never spoke out officially against the Aryan legislation in general." He quoted Proverbs 31:8, which notes, "Speak up for those who canot speak for themselves."

The story of Hitler's day seems so unbelievable. In the pogrom of November 1938, 119 synagogues were set on fire, 20,000 Jews were arrested, shops were looted and prominent Jewish citizens publicly humiliated. That destruction was met with public silence both by the evangelical and Roman Catholic churches of the day. God forbid that we should ever allow ourselves to be silent and not raise a prophetic voice in the day in which we live. We simply cannot allow the state to rule out the opportunity for access to Christian values of life and justice. Silence, at that point, becomes collusion and consent.

This leads to a third alternative: to raise a prophetic voice. There are various ways to do so; so many, in fact, that it is sometimes hard to know which one to choose. If you put them on a continuum, pouring ketchup on Morgentaler might be on one end; being a wimp for Jesus, on the other. How far does the democratic process allow us to go, in being both productive and prophetic? That is a hard question.

It is vital to heed the call to exercise a prophetic ministry in today's world. Failure to heed is to allow our society to self-destruct without ever hearing a word from the Lord. The styles of prophecy will differ. They certainly did so in Old Testament times. Isaiah was comfortable in the king's palace and could conduct himself accordingly. Jeremiah was fated to speak out while his country fell into decline and disaster. But speak out they both did.

One of the best New Testament examples is contained in Paul's letter to Philemon where he expresses his concern about the return of Onesimus the slave. He instructs Philemon to receive him as a brother beloved. He was, at that particular point, teaching Philemon the principles, which, in the end, would make slavery impossible. In this case, Paul's diplomatic skills won out over his reputation for being abrasive.

The New Testament continually modelled this approach in

its attitude toward women, children and justice generally. It was not always as outspoken on these issues as we sometimes might desire, and we cannot always explain why. Was it because New Testament writers gave priority to the gospel, not wanting to become sidetracked by social concerns? Was it because they felt that the end of the world was coming soon, increasing the urgency of preaching the gospel? Or, was it because the church needed to be established before it took on front-line battles of this nature? I would prefer the latter explanation. Whatever the reason, it opted, in many of these situations, for a prophetic voice that proved effective, in the long run.

An excellent example of constructive use of the prophetic voice came out of the famous Clapham Sect. That group consisted of outstanding evangelical Anglicans in Britain, William Wilberforce and Lord Shaftsbury among them. Their work led, eventually, to the freedom of the slaves, the reform of the prison system of that day and the improving of employment standards in the factories. They were able to raise the profile of issues in a way that the general public and the political leaders were able, having seen the urgency, to act on solutions.

The way that the Clapham Sect went about its work was significant. Its members did not, for example, repay evil for evil, but put into practice Romans 12:17 and 18, which encourages, "If it is possible, as far as it depends on you, live at peace with everyone."

They did not, however, purchase peace out of silence. They did it out of love. They exhibited a warm, accepting and cheerful spirit in the days in which they lived, but they did, indeed, raise a prophetic voice. It was a voice which, in the long run, was strikingly effective in gaining acceptance for the reforms it proposed.

We have ample opportunity to do the same in the Christian community. We can do that by direct lobby of political leaders or in public ministry. We can have access to the readers of newspapers—either by writing letters-to-the-editor or by talking to the people who make editorial policy. There are similar means of access to radio and television editorial decision-makers. There has been, over the past period of time, a greater openness on the part of the media to hear the Christian cause, despite the embarassment some Christians in the media bring to us.

It is important to note, that if we are to make a Christian influence felt, we have an additional responsibility to vote our convictions at elections, something at which we have been conspicuously unsuccessful. Strategists in most political parties know that, at election time, we vote party affiliation, not evangelical conviction. That needs to change. At the Canadian government level, little even of lip service, is given to Christian belief and behavior. There is, in fact, no longer a consensus within the church, in the broadest sense, on a number of issues which are important to the evangelical community.

But we do live in a society where Caesar gives us the right to vote, to speak and to contend for what we believe. It may mean that some of us will have to accept that the state will punish us for our convictions. Some of the implications of legislation on sexual orientation may very well lead to that before too long. We must do what we have to, nevertheless, not out of narrow legalism, but out of a love for people, a cheerful heart, a dogged determination and a prophetic commitment. What will happen, we do not know. We may lose all the battles and even the war itself. On the other hand, we may be the very people who, under God, begin to make the society aware of the need for spiritual and community renewal.

Render to Caesar we must. But we must also tell Caesar what God has to say. We must be emphatic and committed in raising our voice. The priorities are always to be set by our faithfulness to the Lord our God.

Printed in the United States
1397700001B/16-30